AMERICAN HERITAGE

April, 1971 • Volume XXII, Number 3

LIBRARY OF CONGRESS

Most of us remember Franklin D. Roosevelt confined to a wheelchair or able to walk about only with the aid of crutches. But in the summer of 1917, when he was thirty-five years old, the Assistant Secretary of the Navy, and not yet a victim of polio, descriptions likened him to a matinee idol.

With the First World War then on, Walter Camp, the famed Yale coach, expressed to F.D.R. his fear that members of the Wilson administration would break under the strain of work unless they got some exercise. Roosevelt immediately urged Camp to come to Washington to set up a physical-conditioning program. Cabinet members as well as their subordinates were invited to participate. However, Roosevelt's boss, Secretary of the Navy Josephus Daniels, took a jaundiced view of the matter. He was in his mid-fifties at the time and had always shunned sports. As his son Jonathan relates in the book *The End of Innocence*, the Secretary, after much badgering from Roosevelt, finally consulted a doctor. "Joe," said the physician, "you never took any exercise in your life. You never walked when you could ride. Stay away from that crowd and you'll live longer."

So, while Daniels grabbed an extra bit of sleep each morning, Roosevelt would leave home at 7:15 to join a hardier crew in jumping, stretching, squatting, and running "double quick" through Potomac Park. (Unfortunately, we cannot identify any of those sturdy bureaucrats with him in the photograph above.) Soon, however, Roosevelt came down with a bad cold and later an infected throat. Josephus Daniels, on the other hand, wasn't out sick a single day during the war, and he outlived all his well-known colleagues, dying at the age of eighty-five in 1948.

AMERICAN HERITAGE

The Magazine of History

Sponsored by
American Association for State & Local History · Society of American Historians

CONTENTS *April, 1971 · Volume XXII, Number 3*

COVER: Man o' War, the most noted of all American thoroughbreds, was a two-year-old and making his astonishing debut at Belmont Park, Long Island, in 1919, when this painting was executed. Johnny Loftus, who rode him in all his starts as a two-year-old, is in the saddle. After a spectacular career on the track, as described in Peter Chew's article on page 24, Man o' War retired to an even more remarkable one at stud, siring many great racers. The painting is in the collection of the National Museum of Racing, Inc., at Saratoga Springs, New York. *Back cover:* For permitting us to reproduce their fine G.A.R. emblem we are indebted to the Hirschl and Adler Galleries in New York City.

AMERICAN HERITAGE is published every two months by American Heritage Publishing Co., Inc.; editorial and executive offices, 551 Fifth Avenue, New York, N.Y. 10017. Treasurer, Marjorie C. Dyer; Secretary, John C. Taylor III. Correspondence about subscriptions should be sent to American Heritage Subscription Office, 383 West Center Street, Marion, Ohio 43302. Single copies: $5.00. Annual subscriptions: $20.00 in U.S. and Canada; $21.00 elsewhere.

A ten-year Index covering Volumes VI–XV is available at $5.00; a new five-year Index of Volumes XVI–XX has just been published at $3.50.

AMERICAN HERITAGE will consider but assumes no responsibility for unsolicited materials. Title registered U.S. Patent Office. Second-class postage paid at New York, N.Y., and at additional mailing offices.

THE FIGHT FOR THE QUEEN, or

OLIVER JENSEN

PRECEDING OVERLEAF: *Seen from Lookout Point above Clarksville, Missouri, the* Delta Queen *heads southward through a glorious Mississippi River landscape. The picture above shows the enormous stern paddlewheel at rest and the calliope blowing clouds of steam.*

PHOTO OVERLEAF, JACK ZEHRT

TWO CHEERS FOR CONGRESS

The wonderfully evocative photograph spread across the two preceding pages has a great deal to say, in the way that pictures do, about America, its heritage, and the importance of historic preservation. And besides all that, it is a good point to begin what starts out as a very unhappy story.

About three in the afternoon of November 2 last, with jazz bands blaring, the steam calliope belting out "Auld Lang Syne," and fireboats playing their great arching streams of muddy Mississippi water, the last river packet in the United States, the steamboat in our photograph, slowed down to tie up at New Orleans in what was then widely heralded as her last and final stop. The paddle-wheel palace *Delta Queen*, eleven days out of St. Paul, Minnesota, eased up toward the Poydras Street wharf while eager hands stretched out to take her lines. In Captain Ernest Wagner's pilothouse, where Mark Twain would have felt at home, the engine telegraph signalled back "all stop." For a moment the mournful steam whistle, in one last mighty blast, drowned out the noise with which Americans handle all great events, happy or otherwise. Cameras flashed, television men scurried about, dignitaries maneuvered for position. The full load of passengers, 189 strong and from twenty different states, began to disappear into the crowd. Reporters interviewed anyone and everyone. History had come again to New Orleans. The steamboat age was over and would be buried in a great burst of sentiment. So everyone thought.

It had been like this ever since the *Delta Queen* left her home port of Cincinnati, heading downstream to Cairo, Illinois, where the Ohio joins the Mississippi. Then this final voyage turned north to St. Paul. The word had spread that the forty-four-year-old steamboat, with her wooden superstructure, stood condemned as a fire hazard by Coast Guard regulations and that Congress had refused to spare her. And so as the *Queen* slipped off downriver from St. Paul and maintained her slow, dignified pace along the shores of state after state, vast crowds turned out. They lined the banks at La Crosse, at Prairie du Chien, Dubuque, Clinton, Davenport and her sister city Rock Island, Burlington, Nauvoo, Hannibal (where Mark Twain grew up watching the steamboats), St. Louis, Memphis —at every stop.

These waving multitudes were not simply steamboat enthusiasts, but the people, often a substantial part of a town's whole population, and they held the children aloft to witness the end of an era. Even the modern young appeared, in groups as usual and clutching signs—but reading, as if they were some sort of incongruous royalists, "SAVE THE QUEEN"! And they would chant her out of sight with those words while the *Queen* would answer bravely on her calliope, white puffs streaming from the steam pipes, the notes of "Dixie" and "On Wisconsin" and "When the Saints Go Marching In" echoing off the banks and drifting across the levees, fields, and swamps.

Very few people in this age of cities, automobiles, and air travel ever really see the secret parts of the rivers that course through the central half of America—the Tennessee, the Ohio, the Cumberland, the Mississippi—and now no one save a few towboat crews, powerboat owners, and duck hunters would see them anymore. Yet between towns the wide water courses seem much as our river-oriented ancestors knew them—long, wild panoramas of woods, low islands, dramatic bluffs. Signs of human hab-

CONTINUED ON PAGE 88

By OLIVER JENSEN

"When the regulars had arrived within eighty or one hundred rods, they, hearing our drum beat, halted, charged their guns, and doubled their ranks, and marched up at quick step."

KOSTI RUOHOMAA—BLACK STAR

Voices of Lexington and Concord

What was it like to actually be there in April, 1775?
This is how the participants, American and British, remembered it

Eyewitness accounts are the raw material of recorded history. Although frequently inexact, since they depend on the subjective impressions of biased observers, they are nevertheless indispensable. When important events have been recalled in words by a number of witnesses or participants, something like the true shape of the past emerges from the obscurity of time, lighted in many dimensions, with one partial light kept in proper balance by another. We begin to see what it must have been like to be there when these things happened.

The following account of the opening battle of the American Revolution was compiled by Richard Wheeler, who is at work on a book that will report the entire war in just this fashion. Entitled Voices of 1776, *it will be published in 1972 by Thomas Y. Crowell Company. Throughout, it has been Mr. Wheeler's effort to choose his quotations first for fidelity to the larger picture, and only second for interest and color, so that the resulting account is as authentic as possible.* —The Editors

Spring's arrival brought little of its usual inspiration to the province of Massachusetts in the year 1775. America's long-standing quarrel with England had reached a point where an explosion seemed imminent, and Massachusetts was the powder keg.

The crisis had been coming on for several years with continuous acceleration. Repeated British efforts to force taxation on the American colonies had evoked violent reactions in incidents now famous—the Boston Massacre (1770), the burning of the customs schooner *Gaspee* (1772), the Boston Tea Party (1773). The First Continental Congress, meeting in Philadelphia late in 1774, consolidated American opinion against Britain's coercive measures. Tough economic reprisals against the mother country were agreed to, as well as preparations for armed resistance should all else fail. So it was that the spring of 1775 resounded to drum and fife, especially in Massachusetts, as men of all ages, wearing homespun breeches and gripping worn muskets, trained under graying veterans of the French and Indian War.

General Thomas Gage, the military governor of Massachusetts, was under heavy pressure to put the upstart colonials in their place. In mid-April he decided to send a force of about 750 men to seize and destroy large quantities of military supplies that his spies reported at Concord, about twenty miles from Boston. Along the route an advance patrol was to try to capture John Hancock and Samuel Adams, two of the most prominent Patriot leaders, who were lodged in nearby Lexington.

But the Patriots of Boston had a spy system that was just as good as Gage's.

Paul Revere relates:

In the fall of 1774 and winter of 1775, I was one of upwards of thirty . . . who formed ourselves into a committee for the purpose of watching the movements of the British soldiers, and gaining every intelligence of the movements of the Tories. We held our meetings at the Green Dragon Tavern [in Boston]. We were so careful that our meetings should be kept secret that every time we met, every person swore upon the Bible that they would not discover any of our transactions but to Messrs. Hancock, Adams, Doctors [Joseph] Warren, [Benjamin] Church and one or two more. . . . In the winter, towards the spring, we frequently took turns, two and two, to watch the soldiers by patrolling the streets all night.

The Saturday night preceding the 19th of April, about twelve o'clock at night, the boats belonging to the transports were all launched [from shore] and carried under the sterns of the men-of-war. (They had been previously hauled up and repaired.) We likewise found that the grenadiers and light infantry were all taken off duty. From these movements we expected something serious was to be transacted. On Tuesday evening, the 18th, it was observed that a number of soldiers were marching towards the bottom of the Common. About ten o'clock, Dr. Warren sent in great haste for me and begged that I would immediately set off for Lexington, where Messrs. Hancock and Adams were, and acquaint them of the movement, and that it was thought they were the objects. When I got to Dr. Warren's house, I found he had sent an express by land to Lexington—a Mr. William Dawes.

The Sunday before, by desire of Dr. Warren, I had been to Lexington, to Messrs. Hancock and Adams, who were at the Rev. Mr. Clark's. I returned at night through

By RICHARD WHEELER

"...the British were then at the bridge.... Captain Davis returned to his company and drew his sword, and said to the company, 'I haven't a man that is afraid to go,' and gave the word 'March!'"

KOSTI RUOHOMAA—BLACK STAR

Charlestown; there I agreed with a Colonel Conant and some other gentlemen that if the British went out by water, we [in Boston] would show two lanthorns in the North Church steeple; and if by land, one as a signal; for we were apprehensive it would be difficult [for a messenger] to cross the Charles River or get over Boston Neck.

I left Dr. Warren, called upon a friend and desired him to make the signals. I then went home, took my boots and surtout, went to the north part of the town, where I kept a boat; two friends rowed me across Charles River, a little to the eastward where the *Somerset* man of war lay. It was then young flood, the ship was winding, and the moon was rising. They landed me on the Charlestown side. When I got into town, I met Colonel Conant and several others; they said they had seen our signals. I told them what was acting. . . .

I set off upon a very good horse; it was then about eleven o'clock and very pleasant. After I had passed Charlestown Neck . . . I saw two men on horseback under a tree. When I got near them, I discovered they were British officers. One tried to get ahead of me, and the other to take me. I turned my horse very quick and galloped toward Charlestown Neck, and then pushed for the Medford road. The one who chased me, endeavoring to cut me off, got into a clay pond. . . . I got clear of him, and went through Medford, over the bridge, and up to Menotomy [now Arlington]. In Medford, I awakened the captain of the minute men; and after that I alarmed almost every house, till I got to Lexington.

The people of Lexington already suspected that something momentous was stirring. Among the first to take the alarm had been Orderly Sergeant William Munroe, of the militia company commanded by Captain John Parker:

. . . Early in the evening of the 18th of . . . April, I was informed by Solomon Brown, who had just returned from Boston, that he had seen nine British officers on the road, travelling leisurely, sometimes before and sometimes behind him; that he had discovered, by the occasional blowing aside of their topcoats, that they were armed. On learning this, I supposed they had some design upon Hancock and Adams, who were then at the house of the Rev. Mr. Clarke, and immediately assembled a guard of eight men, with their arms, to guard the house.

About midnight, Col. Paul Revere rode up and requested admittance. I told him the family had just retired, and had requested that they might not be disturbed by any noise about the house.

"Noise!" said he. "You'll have noise enough before long. The regulars are coming out."

We then permitted him to pass. Soon after, [another messenger] came. These gentlemen came different routes . . . and both brought letters from Dr. Warren in Boston to Hancock and Adams, stating that a large body of British troops had left Boston, and were on their march to Lexington.

According to Lieutenant John Barker, of the King's Own, the British expedition had trouble getting started:

. . . Between 10 and 11 o'clock all the Grenadiers and Light Infantry of the army . . . (under the command of Lt. Col. Smith of the 10th and Major Pitcairn of the Marines), embarked and were landed upon the opposite shore on Cambridge Marsh. Few but the commanding officers knew what expedition we were going upon. After getting over the marsh, where we were wet up to the knees, we were halted in a dirty road and stood there [for a long time] waiting for provisions to be brought from the boats and to be divided, and which most of the men threw away, having carried some with 'em.

Ensign Jeremy Lister, of the 10th Regiment of Foot, adds:

We . . . was on our march by one, which was at first through some swamps and slips of the sea till we got into the road leading to Lexington, soon after which the country people begun to fire their alarm guns [and] light their beacons, to raise the country. . . .

Soon after midnight, Paul Revere and William Dawes had ridden from Lexington toward Concord, spreading the alarm as they went. They were shortly overtaken by a young doctor named Samuel Prescott, a Concord man who had been in Lexington visiting his sweetheart. He decided to aid them in their mission. Ahead of the riders were the British officers who were patrolling in advance of the main body. The officers had in custody three Lexington men: Elijah Sanderson, Solomon Brown, and Jonathan Loring. The trio had been captured while trying to keep the patrol under surveillance. Sanderson says:

It was a bright moon-light. . . . During our detention, they put many questions to us, which I evaded. They kept us separately, and treated us very civilly. They particularly inquired where Hancock and Adams were; also about the population. . . . While we were under detention, they took . . . Col. Paul Revere. . . .

Revere explains:

We had got nearly half way; Mr. Dawes and the doctor stopped to alarm the people of a house; I was about one hundred rods ahead, when I saw two men, in nearly the same situation as those officers were near Charlestown. I called for the doctor and Mr. Dawes to come up; in an instant I was surrounded by four;—they had placed themselves in a straight road that inclined each way; they had taken down a pair of bars on the north side of the road, and two of them were under a tree in the pasture.

The doctor being foremost, he came up; and we tried

"We then saw the whole body a coming out of town.
We were ordered to lay behind a wall that run over a hill, and when they got nigh enough, Major Buttrick said he would give the word fire."

KOSTI RUOHOMAA—BLACK STAR

to get past them; but they being armed with pistols and swords, they forced us into the pasture; the doctor jumped his horse over a low stone wall, and got to Concord. I observed a wood at a small distance, and made for that. When I got there, out started six officers on horseback, and ordered me to dismount.

William Dawes was by this time escaping back toward Lexington. Sanderson resumes:

They brought [Revere] within half a rod of me, and I heard him speak up with energy to them, "Gentlemen, you've missed of your aim!"

One said, rather hardly, "What of our aim?"

Revere replied, "I came out of Boston an hour after your toops had come out of Boston and landed at Lechmere's Point; and if I had not known people had been sent out to give information to the country, and time enough to get fifty miles, I would have ventured one shot from you before I would have suffered you to have stopped me."

Upon this, they went a little aside and conversed together. They then ordered me to untie my horse (which was tied to a little birch) and mount. They kept us in the middle of the road, and rode on each side of us. We went toward Lexington. They took all of us (Revere, Loring, and Brown, and myself). My horse not being swift, and they riding at considerable speed, one of the officers pressed my horse forward by striking him with his hanger.

When we had arrived within fifty or one hundred rods of the meeting-house, Loring . . . told them, "The bell's a ringing, the town's alarmed, and you're all dead men!"

They then stopped—conferred together. One of them dismounted, and ordered me to dismount, and said to me, "I must do you an injury." I asked what he was going to do to me now. He made no reply, but with his hanger cut my bridle and girth. . . .

The same was done to the horses belonging to Loring and Brown, and all three of the Lexington men were released. Revere was still in custody as the ride was resumed. A moment later, some gunfire was heard in the village—possibly an alarm volley by the assembling militia. The British stopped again, and Revere noted that they were now greatly concerned:

The major inquired of me how far it was to Cambridge, and if there were any other road. After some consultation, the major rode up to the sergeant and asked if his horse was tired. He answered him he was. . . . "Then," said he, "take that man's horse." I dismounted, and the sergeant mounted my horse. . . .

The British rode off, leaving Revere standing on the moonlit road. He watched them go quickly past the meeting house and back toward Cambridge, seemingly intent on joining the main expedition. Then:

I went across the burying-ground and some pastures, and came to the Rev. Mr. Clark's house, where I found Messrs. Hancock and Adams. I told them of my treatment, and they concluded to go from that house towards Woburn. I went with them. . . .

According to Orderly Sergeant Munroe, who provided the party's military escort:

To [taking flight] Hancock consented with great reluctance. . . . I however conducted them to the north part of the town, and then returned. . . . I found Capt. Parker and his militia company paraded on the common, a little in the rear of the meeting-house. About that time, one of our messengers, who had been sent toward Cambridge to get information of the movement of the regulars, returned and reported that he could not learn that there were any troops on the road from Boston to Lexington, which raised some doubt as to their coming. . . .

Militiaman Ebenezer Munroe takes up the narrative:

The weather being rather chilly, after calling the roll, we were dismissed, but ordered to remain within call of the drum. The men generally went into the tavern adjoining the common. . . .

The last person sent [toward Cambridge] was Thaddeus Bowman, who returned between daylight and sunrise and informed Capt. Parker that the British troops were within a mile of the meeting-house. Capt. Parker immediately ordered the drum beat to arms. I was the first that followed the drum. I took my station on the right of our line, which was formed from six to ten rods back of the meeting-house, facing south.

About seventy of our company had assembled when the British troops appeared. Some of our men went into the meeting-house, where the town's powder was kept. . . . When the regulars had arrived within eighty or one hundred rods, they, hearing our drum beat, halted, charged their guns, and doubled their ranks, and marched up at quick step.

Capt. Parker ordered his men to stand their ground, and not to molest the regulars unless they meddled with us.

There is reason to think that Parker's simply worded order was somewhat romanticized for history by his grandson, who reported it as: "Stand your ground. Don't fire unless fired upon. But if they mean to have a war, let it begin here." Ebenezer Munroe continues:

The British troops came up directly in our front. The commanding officer advanced within a few rods of us and exclaimed, "Disperse, you damned rebels! You dogs, run!—Rush on, my boys!" and fired his pistol.

The British version of the encounter's opening is different. In the

CONTINUED ON PAGE 98

Indians still camp beside Buffalo Creek in this romantic view of Lake Erie painted about 1810. The ships in the distance are anchored off Fort Erie. The painting is attributed to Edward Walsh, a British army surgeon. That may be he sketching in the foreground.

THE LEGEND OF A LAKE

By FRANKLIN RUSSELL

The lake was liberated from glacial ice ten thousand years before Babylon was built. Thus, it had more than fifteen thousand years in which to transform from an almost sterile, ice-gouged river valley into fecund, prosperous Lake Erie.

In fifteen millennia the lake received more than ninety species of fish and immense and varied populations of insects, worms, and crustaceans, and built up the largest concentrations of freshwater fish in the world.

However, the real story of Lake Erie is always overwhelmed by the many superlatives surrounding it. The lake exemplifies a great theme: man taming nature. It is the dramatic centerpiece of awesome industrial power. It is the reason for a great gathering of human beings—from a few-score thousands in 1800 to more than thirteen million today. Its history is filled with tales of great disasters, of shipwrecks and vicious storms, of murderous fogs and floods, while its waters have yielded more than a million tons of fish. It is, most recently, the publicized victim in a story of human sewage and industrial poisons.

None of these stories, separately or in concert, make real sense of the lake. To do so, it is necessary to invoke the legendary lake—a lake that cannot be truly measured or recorded—and watch its transformation, its many biological agonies, as it passes from the primeval to the civilized. This is the real story, hidden from the view of most men, and it ends in the most revealing of all superlatives.

Erie is a young lake, born of the last ice age, which began its retreat about twenty thousand years ago. The melting ice filled the basin, and the surrounding drainage system sent in phosphorus and nitrogen, which provided a setting for aquatic plants and animals. Aquatic insects followed close behind the retreating ice.

The larval forms of these insects thrived in icy-cold water. They fastened eggs to stones in brooks tumbling with ice pans and found refuge in gravel or in mud. The greatest of these insects were the mayflies. They had a long history of success, dating from before the arrival of grass or flowering plants. Their night-dancing hordes blotted out the moon's light, and rains of eggs dropped into the lake, creating an almost-unlimited supply of larval food for the fish that were coming.

The migrants poured into the lake and the rivers and streams around it. Brook trout, lake trout, and northern suckers found the cold water ideal. Following them came yellow walleyes and blue pike, drums and carpsuckers, saugers and ciscoes, lake sturgeon and muskellunge. Each fish found its special place in the lake. The sturgeon prowled the bottom and grazed on mussels and snails. The giant muskellunge, cut off from the Mississippi drainage system, frequented shallow aquatic plant meadows along the lake's shores and swam up rivers to spawn in swamps. The ciscoes hunted microscopic plants and animals below the surface and along the bottom. The pike and sauger chased the ciscoes. The yellow walleye hunted in shady shallows and spawned in rushing streams or the lake itself.

The immigrant fish found an exceptionally hospitable home in the nearly ten thousand square miles of Erie. The lake was shallow throughout its 240-mile length, averaging less than sixty feet in depth. A flat-bottomed central basin was separated from a shallow western basin by a rocky island chain. The deepest basin, in the east, was separated from the central basin by a ridge of sand and gravel. These basins were great places for spawning, and the fish gathered by the millions. Their eggs dropped into holes in the dolomitic and limestone rock or lodged amid the gravel at the bottom, secure from egg-hunters.

Unlike Lake Superior to the north, which lay in a tough bowl of very ancient rock, Erie sat uneasily in a shifting disintegration of its shores. Instead of rock strands, it was surrounded by silty clay, and much of its shoreline was so weak it was constantly collapsing. Quick-rising western winds whipped up waves that nibbled away fifteen hundred acres of land every year. But for the lake creatures this was ideal. The collapsing shores created marshlands and shoreline havens of wild rice and aquatic plants. Great plant growths choked estuaries and bays. Fish bred there, too, and wildfowl came to mate and rest.

The fish bounty of Lake Erie and its environs was a legacy of the withdrawn ice. Ohio, in particular, abounded with springs, some bubbling from the tops of hills. From these springs spread a network of deep, narrow, clear-water streams and rivers winding away toward the Ohio and the Mississippi river systems, running into the Maumee and the Sandusky, the Vermilion and the Cuyahoga, and all the other rivers linked, one way or another, with Lake Erie.

The first Europeans watched, disbelieving, as the fish hordes rushed upriver to spawn, teemed in the lake shallows, and collected by the thousands in pools and lagoons. They hunted them with spears, pitchforks, axes, nets, guns. The soldiers of a fort built on the banks of the Maumee fished each afternoon, and it was a poor day when they did not get a thousand fish. The fish collected so thickly in pools below some rapids that it was said a blindfolded man could toss a spear and get a fish nine times out of ten.

So great was the abundance of fish and fresh water that land and lake were not at first affected by the flood of settlers from the East. These eager, impatient pioneers carved fortunes from the primeval landscape. They felled an estimated twenty-five million acres of forest in fifty years. They built hundreds of dams, placing them across any river strong enough to provide water-wheel power. An 8-foot-high dam, built across the St. Marys River in 1821, backed up such a crush of migrating yellow walleyes, muskellunge, pike, bass, and suckers in the race waters flanking the dam that men dropped nets, hats, and bare hands into the race and scooped out tons of fish.

The dams destroyed the runs of the spawning fish. Some fish took to spawning in the mouths of rivers or in the lake itself. The big muskies and sturgeon, often killed with axes and hayforks when they were caught in streams too narrow for them to turn around in, found all migration to spawn blocked and remained in the lake. There, fouled in fishing gear, they were slaughtered by the thousands to protect valuable equipment. The beaches of Erie were strewn with their abandoned bodies. The sturgeon that were not fed to hogs were stacked in upright piles on the lake shores by the fishermen and set on fire. The sturgeon did not breed until they were about twenty years old, but their extremely long life—about one hundred years—enabled them to remain in the lake until recently, when all their river spawning-routes were

IDYLLIC LAKE ERIE BEFORE DOOM SET IN

Picturesque America

An 1872 vista from a crumbling bluff near Cleveland inadvertently shows the erosion that silted Erie's waters.

Buffalo, the terminus of the Erie Canal, was a busy port for the transshipment of goods to and from the west via Lake Erie. In the 1871

ALBRIGHT-KNOX ART GALLERY, BUFFALO

painting above by Lars G. Sellstedt, two horses tow a cargo-laden barge to the Porter Avenue pier, while a steamboat gets up smoke.

blocked off. The muskellunge, suffering a somewhat similar fate, were apparently able to spawn in the mouths of some rivers and perpetuate some semblance of their former numbers. But in the early twentieth century, men found these great fish milling together in Maumee Bay in futile gathering for a spawning run that could never begin. Between 1902 and 1905 the men caught up to one hundred muskellunge a day until the big fish were all but wiped out.

The lake and the land around it could accept the build-up of the men and their works to a fixed point. This point was reached by the middle of the nineteenth century. In 1800 there were forty-five thousand Ohioans and an estimated thirty thousand New Yorkers, Pennsylvanians, and Canadians clustered around the lake. By 1850 the number of Ohioans had swelled to nearly two million. A flood of silt began—farmers' topsoil leached from hillsides or from under the tramping feet of hundreds of thousands of cattle. Clay was torn from stream banks and ripped from rivers made suddenly violent in their floods by the disappearance of the great spongy network of tree roots in the fallen forests.

Sewage from hundreds of towns and villages joined the silt flow, along with effluents from tanneries, breweries, chemical works, oil wells, and mines. They were joined by blizzards of sawdust from lumber mills. Flood waters ran yellow, gray, black. The fabled Ohio springs began to dry up.

By 1875 industrious Irishmen and then Germans had drained the Black Swamp and turned it into a huge vegetable garden. While they prospered, millions of tons of rich black earth began the journey into Lake Erie from the crumbling soft banks of the farmers' drainage ditches and from the ceaseless activity of their plows.

It now scarcely mattered that many waterpowered machines lay idle in summer, when streams diminished to a trickle. Steam power now drove the machines. Steam power sent fishermen into Lake Erie, and by the late nineteenth century they were winching in more than twenty thousand tons of fish a year. Steam power demonstrated a new mastery of nature. New dams and reservoirs now stemmed the flood waters. Rivers were straightened and channels dredged. When the valuable Erie stocks of whitefish and ciscoes began declining, the men ingeniously perfected methods of artificially propagating whitefish, trout, ciscoes, pike, and smallmouth bass. Hundreds of millions of fingerlings were released into the lake, and another triumph of the new technology seemed complete.

However, it soon became clear that brute power and ingenuity were not quite enough to bring this man-dominated world of lake and land to order. Unaccountably, the millions of artificially propagated fish never grew to fill the fishermen's nets. The men theorized that perhaps

A popular resort before the turn of the century, Put-in-Bay (right), near Sandusky, Ohio, was dotted with exclusive hotels that catered to millionaires and statesmen, until the hotels burned down and the nabobs bought themselves private islands nearby. Below, groups of strollers in holiday best view Cleveland from atop the parapet of the city's first reservoir, built in 1856. The wall was thirty-five feet above street level and commanded a splendid prospect of the city and the lake.

Picturesque America

WESTERN RESERVE HISTORICAL SOCIETY, CLEVELAND

Picturesque America

OLD PRINT SHOP, NEW YORK

END OF THE IDYLL

Lake steamers and sail of every rig crowd the waterfront of Detroit (left) in this 1872 view from the pastoral serenity of the Canadian side of the Detroit River near where it flows into Lake Erie. At about the same time, the already unsightly riverbank at Toledo, Ohio (below), on the western side of the Maumee River less than a dozen miles from the lake, was bristling with small factories. Besides offending the eye, these little industries were already dumping their wastes into the water and helping to upset the balance of life beneath the surface of the once-beautiful Lake Erie.

there was something wrong with the propagation process, but the lake itself suggested another explanation.

In 1881, when the superintendent of the Ohio fish hatcheries was collecting whitefish eggs in the western basin reefs and rocks for propagation, he saw the spawning whitefish driven away by a vast blanket of silt flushed into the lake by a cloudburst on land. The silt settled, in places covering the spawning reefs and gravel completely.

During the late nineteenth century, in every spring and fall downpour, the silt became an enveloping submarine blizzard that rolled out into Lake Erie from every river and stream. In the original balance of the lake, the spring blooming of plankton came just when trillions of fish eggs were hatching, and the young fish fed on the plankton. But the sun could not penetrate these murky waters. Great spring crops of diatoms, single-celled globular plants, once a mainstay fish food in the western basin, were obliterated. Plankton-loving ciscoes were driven east. Whitefish eggs smothered in the reef refuges. Yellow walleyes, which used to rush upriver as soon as the ice had gone, were checked and driven back into the lake without spawning.

Gradually the silt storms smothered most of the shoreline aquatic vegetation that had been a refuge for all kinds of wildlife—waterfowl, aquatic insects, amphibians, and spawning fish. The lake's western basin held between three hundred and five hundred thousand tons of silt in suspension at almost any time. The eggs of some yellow walleyes that spawned on gravel bottoms were smothered by the silt. Others, which still sought spawning grounds up rivers, were stopped by chemicals or by sawdust that compacted in their gills, and they were driven back into the lake to wander in search of new places to spawn.

But even in the lake there was little chance to escape the rush of displaced earth into the water. The yellow walleyes had spent generations habituating themselves to dim light. They would eat only at sunrise and sunset when the light was soft enough for them to hunt. Then they went after perch, minnows, and suckers. But the gathering silt, some of it so fine it was suspended in the water for months, clouded the lake. The yellow walleyes could not see well enough to hunt and left their traditional spawning grounds.

Hit by the sun, the particles of silt absorbed and retained heat, turning large areas of the lake into a kind of vast heat sponge. Some particles, decaying, actually produced heat. At the same time, heavily wooded streams lost their shade, and aquatic meadows everywhere were stripped away. The sun poured down on unshaded water everywhere. In the 1920's an extremely hot summer drove the ciscoes into the deepest part of the central basin, and there they concentrated in immense numbers. There, also, the fishermen found them, and their eager nets caught ciscoes by the billions.

CONTINUED ON PAGE 76

The "Mostest Hoss"

Concerning the long life, fast times, and astonishing fecundity of Man o' War

In 1920 William T. Waggoner of Fort Worth, Texas, possessed a string of racehorses, hundreds of thousands of acres of prime cattle land dotted with oil wells, and the firm conviction, apparently born of experience, that everything has a price. That year a lustrous chestnut colt was running away from the nation's best three-year-olds with ridiculous ease, and it occurred to Waggoner that this colt was the greatest thoroughbred that he or any other American horseman had ever seen or was ever likely to see. Waggoner wanted him in the worst way, and he offered $500,000 to the colt's owner, Samuel D. Riddle, of Glen Riddle, Pennsylvania.

Riddle had paid $5,000 for the colt at the Saratoga Yearling Sales and had long since reached the same conclusion about him. Riddle rejected the Texan's offer.

Waggoner must have been prepared for the initial rebuff. A textile manufacturer, Riddle was, after all, a wealthy man too. But Riddle was a Scot, a near man with a dollar. Playing upon this weakness, Waggoner raised his offer to $1,000,000. Again, Riddle turned him down.

"Well, how much then?" asked Waggoner.

"The colt is not for sale," insisted Riddle.

Waggoner signed a blank check and gave it to him.

MRS. ELLSWORTH H. AUGUSTUS

This stallion, painted by T. Percy Earl, is the reason for owner Samuel D. Riddle's grin. He is Man o' War, Clarence Kummer up, at Belmont Park in 1920, when races were still run clockwise.

By PETER CHEW

KEENELAND LIBRARY

"You go to France," said Riddle, "and bring back the sepulchre of Napoleon from Les Invalides. Then you go to England and buy the jewels from the crown. Then to India and buy the Taj Mahal. Then I'll put a price on Man o' War."

Man o' War was truly a horse without price. As no other horse before or since, he fired the imagination of the American public. When he came upon the scene as a two-year-old in 1919, thoroughbred racing was suffering. Antigambling legislation inspired by Governor Charles Evans Hughes had closed down racing completely in New York in 1911 and 1912, and a number of other states had followed suit. Many of the smaller stables had liquidated their stock, the big stables had shipped their horses to race in Europe, and the bottom had fallen out of the thoroughbred yearling market. No sooner had the ban been lifted, and the racetracks reopened, than World War I loomed. In 1919, purses and attendance were at record lows.

But once Man o' War began racing, his name on a track program was certain to fill the grandstand. In time, policemen had to be assigned to prevent souvenir hunters from snatching hairs from his mane and tail, and his thundering hoofs became as much a part of the Golden Age of Sports as the crack of Babe Ruth's bat or Bill Tilden's whistling serves.

Man o' War looked the part of a superhorse. At two he was lithe and leggy. At three he filled out into a magnificent animal, standing nearly 16.2 hands (about five and a half feet) at the withers, weighing 1,100 pounds, with a 72-inch girth. He had keenly alert eyes, flaring nostrils, and a white star on his forehead.

"Even when he was standing motionless in his stall with his ears pricked forward and his eyes focused on something slightly above the horizon which mere people never see, energy poured from him," wrote sportswriter Joe H. Palmer. "He could get in no position which suggested actual repose, and his very stillness was that of the coiled spring, of the crouched tiger."

John Hervey, a turf historian, saw Man o' War as a horse "of heroic proportions with no surplus flesh anywhere." Watching him in the paddock at Belmont Park, Long Island, before the running of the Withers Mile in

The man who masterminded Man o' War's breeding was financier August Belmont II, who was photographed under a parasol with Mrs. John Sanford at Saratoga in 1914. At her left is her husband, a heavy bettor on favorites. "Big Red" was descended from the Godolphin Arabian, a founder of the thoroughbred line in the eighteenth century. In the painting by George Stubbs (left), Godolphin's stablemate, a cat called Grimalkin, poses beside the barn door. Man o' War's sire, peering from his stall (center), was the volatile Fair Play. His dam (right) was the gentle Mahubah.

BELOW, LEFT TO RIGHT: COLLECTION OF E. J. ROUSUCK; UPI; KEENELAND LIBRARY

MAN O' WAR'S RECORD AS A SIRE

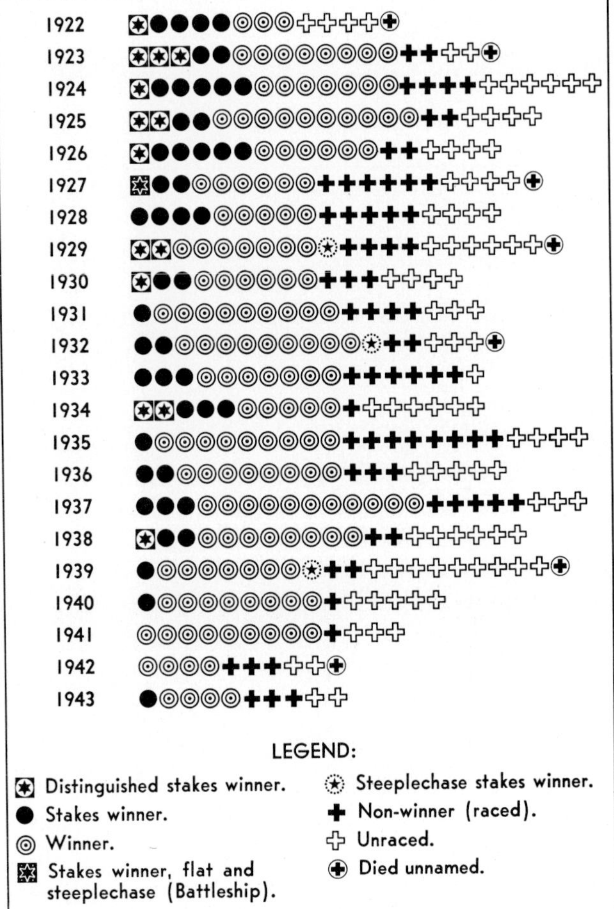

The Blood-Horse

In his more than twenty years at stud, Man o' War sired an impressive number of offspring. Although none ever reached the stature of their father, many became well-known racehorses in their own right, among them War Admiral, American Flag, Mars, Crusader, War Glory, War Relic, Clyde Van Dusen, and Scapa Flow. Perhaps the most successful of all was Battleship, a stakes winner in flat racing who later became a steeplechaser and in 1938 won the world's highest honor in this field, the Grand National Steeplechase in England. The chart above, prepared for The Blood-Horse *magazine by Joe Estes, indicates the record of all of Man o' War's progeny. The horses are grouped by the year in which they were foaled. Of the 386 registered foals Man o' War sired, seven died before they were named and ninety never raced. Of the remaining 289 horses, sixty-nine raced without winning, but 220 were winners, and sixty-one of these won stakes races on flat tracks. Besides Battleship, three other offspring of Man o' War were steeplechase stakes winners. At right is one of thirteen foals he sired in 1922, his first year at stud.*

1920, Hervey wrote, "His beautiful head with its long star was held proudly and the long sinewy neck was curved like that of a war horse. The powerful quarters with their great bunches of muscles were the acme of power. . . ."

Quick, powerful, and fiery as he was, "Big Red," as he was nicknamed, was nevertheless amenable in the stable. He did have his idiosyncrasies, however. He was a prodigious "doer," as horsemen say, consuming great quantities of oats and hay. To thwart his tendency to bolt his feed, his groom, Frank Loftus, placed a bit in his mouth at mealtime.

When feeling frisky, Man o' War would steal up behind his exercise boy, Clyde Gordon, snatch his hat in his teeth, and prance around his stall with it in a game of "keep away." At times he showed signs of anxiety. When lying down he sometimes bit his hoofs, an equine habit similar to chewing one's nails. To help quiet him down, a big hunter named Major Treat was placed in a stall next to him, and to ease Big Red's jitters on race days, Gordon would mount Major Treat and accompany Man o' War to the paddock and thence to the post. Man o' War developed such a strong attachment to Major Treat that if he returned to his stall after a workout or a race and found Major Treat gone, he would snort angrily and slam the walls of his stall with his hoofs.

Even with Major Treat in attendance, Man o' War radiated tension in the saddling enclosure before a race, buck-jumping until his trainer, Louis Feustel, gave his girth a final tightening. The hum of the grandstand and the music of the band had a tonic effect upon Big Red as he headed postward with Major Treat alongside. But near the post, after Major Treat had slipped away, the great horse lunged and reared in his anxiety to run, sometimes breaking through the webbing barrier time and time again until it was sprung by the starter.

Once a race was under way, Man o' War never proved a serious problem for jockey Johnny Loftus (no relation to groom Frank Loftus), who rode him in all ten of his two-year-old races, or for Clarence Kummer, his rider in all but two of his races at three. Earl Sande, who rode Big Red only once, was amazed at the way he ran.

"I never felt anything under me like that colt in my life," gasped Sande in the winner's circle after the Miller Stakes at Saratoga in the summer of 1920. "Why, he is a regular machine! He

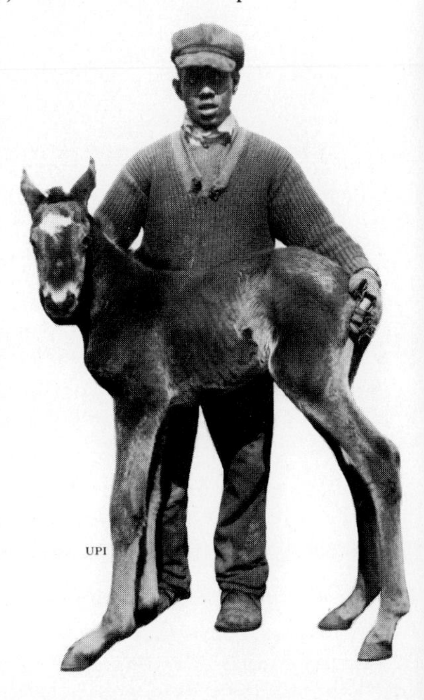

MRS. WALTER M. JEFFORDS, JR.

Noted horse painter Martin Stainforth captured Man o' War's majesty in this 1938 painting. Stud groom Will Harbut holds the reins.

strides farther than anything I ever rode and does it so handily you wouldn't think he was running at all! He is the greatest horse I have ever ridden."

Man o' War was foaled on March 29, 1917, at the Nursery Stud of August Belmont II in the Bluegrass Country outside Lexington, Kentucky. Belmont had inherited his passion for racing and breeding from his father, a millionaire financier for whom Belmont Park and the Belmont Stakes were named.

August Belmont II served on New York State's first racing commission and helped found the Jockey Club, racing's governing body, which he ruled firmly for twenty-nine years, until his death in 1924. John E. Madden, one of this country's most successful breeders of thoroughbreds, considered Belmont the most astute student of bloodlines he had ever known. It was Madden who said that the secret of producing racehorses is to "breed the best to the best—and hope for the best."

Madden's formula is as good as any, and it is how Belmont produced his equine masterpiece, combining as he

CONTINUED ON PAGE 90

"MAD JACK" and the MISSIONARIES

The Pacific Ocean is vast and lonely. In the second decade of the nineteenth century, when the American whaling industry was expanding rapidly in that great sea and American merchant ships plied the lucrative China trade, they ventured in an area where no nation's law extended. The United States naval force in the Pacific totalled at most three vessels, all well occupied in protecting American interests on the coasts of Peru and Chile in the midst of Bolivar's revolution.

This situation was an invitation to the strong and ruthless. Whalers and traders commonly lost men by desertion at the islands and had to recruit their crews from men who had deserted from other ships. Deeds of violence were not uncommon, but the worst to date was the bloody mutiny aboard the American whaleship *Globe*.

Hiram Bingham and his wife, Sybil, by Samuel F. B. Morse

YALE UNIVERSITY ART GALLERY, GIFT OF THE HON. HIRAM BINGHAM

Globe had sailed from Nantucket in December, 1822. One year later, on her second call at the Sandwich Islands (now Hawaii), six of her men deserted and one was discharged. *Globe*'s captain, Thomas Worth, filled out his crew with seven men "from the beach" at Oahu. The ship was not more than a month at sea when, on the night of January 25, 1824, four of these men joined Samuel Comstock, a boatsteerer, in seizing *Globe* and murdering her four officers. The mutineers, with the remainder of the crew afraid to defy them, took the ship to the Mulgrave Islands (now Mili Atoll), where they arrived on February 14. Three days later Comstock was killed by his fellow mutineers. That night, six crewmen who were not involved in the mutiny cut *Globe*'s cable and escaped. They left nine men behind on the island, five of whom were nonmutineers. None of the men on *Globe* was a navigator, but after four months of wandering the ship made Valparaiso. There the United States consul, Michael Hogan, interviewed the sailors and, after manning *Globe* with a new crew, sent the six men home aboard her to stand trial. The men were exonerated, but the story they told when *Globe* returned to Nantucket in November, 1824, set off an outcry for punishment of the mutineers and for protection of American vessels in the Pacific. The citizens of Nantucket and New Bedford petitioned first the outgoing President, James Monroe, and then his successor, John Quincy Adams, for an increased naval force in the Pacific and for a warship to visit the Sandwich Islands. The latter request was seconded by American merchants trading at the islands, who were experiencing difficulty in collecting their debts from the native rulers.

As a result, Commodore Isaac Hull, commanding the

By LINDA McKEE

Hell broke loose in Honolulu when Captain Percival gave his men shore leave in 1826

American squadron in the Pacific, ordered the schooner *Dolphin* to prepare for a cruise among the islands. Her first mission was to visit the Mulgraves and collect any of *Globe*'s men who might still be there; her second was to call at the Sandwich Islands, try to put some curb on desertions there, and do whatever could be done to help the merchants and whalers at Honolulu. Since no American warship had yet visited those islands, Hull ordered *Dolphin*'s commander, Lieutenant John Percival, to learn something of their government and its attitude toward the United States, and to find out whether American vessels were being granted the same privileges as those of other nations.

Dolphin's commander was the very person of the sea dog. Massachusetts-born, Percival had gone to sea at thirteen, been impressed into the Royal Navy, and escaped to join the American service in time for the quasi-war with France. Demobilized in the peace establishment of 1801, he returned to the merchant service, where he earned a remarkable reputation for feats of seamanship including—or so he claimed—the navigation of a ship from Africa to Pernambuco, Brazil, with his entire crew sick or dead of fever.

In 1809 Percival rejoined the American Navy and once again, during the War of 1812, came up "through the hawse-hole" from sailing master to lieutenant. He and Hull had become friends while serving together at Boston, and in 1823 Percival went out as first lieutenant of Hull's flagship, *United States*, leaving a new bride at home. In the Pacific he took command of *Dolphin*. John Percival was then forty-four years old. Although an affable man under most circumstances, he was fiery tempered. His rages, quickly triggered and as quickly ended, had earned him the name of "Mad Jack" or "Crazy Jack" among the sailors. He was a great favorite with the men, who accepted his swearing as a mark of affection; he shared the cabin wines with the sick, and when there were fresh provisions to be distributed, the men on the gun deck shared equally with the officers.

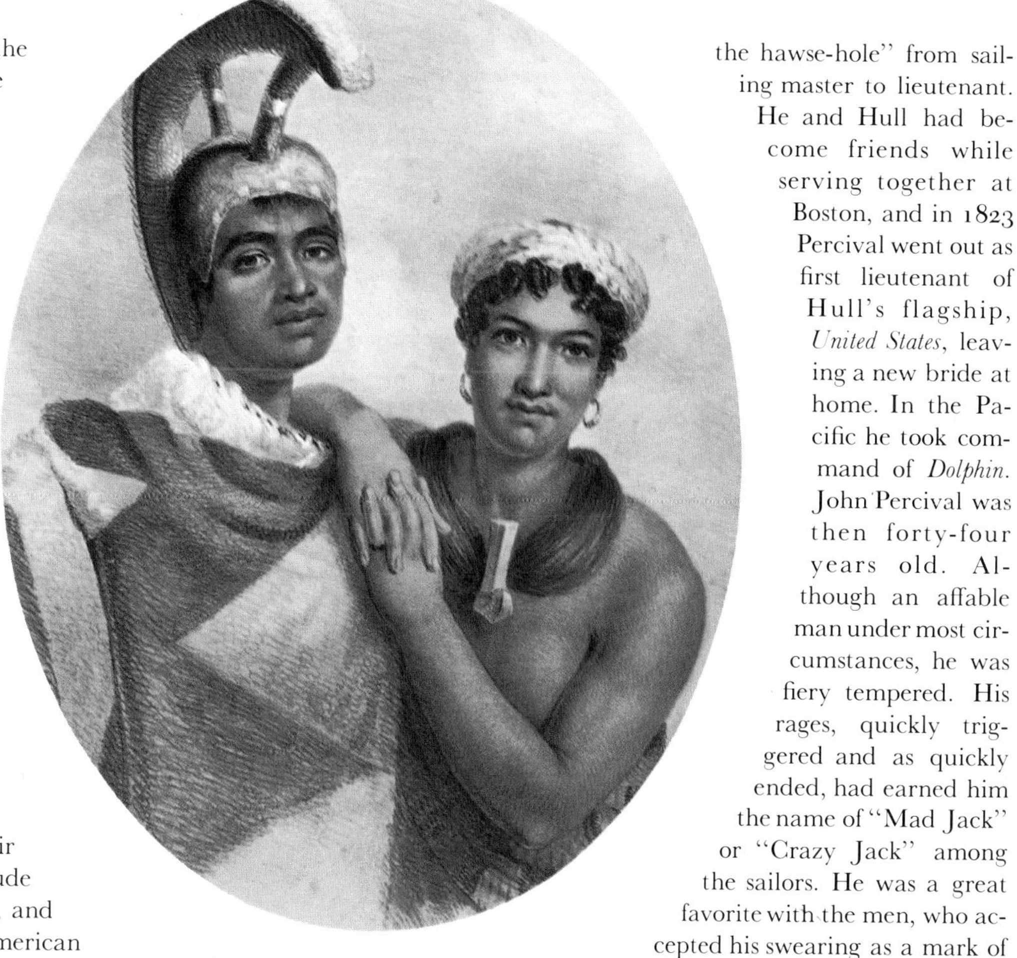

The governor of Oahu, Boki, and his wife, Liliha, by John Hayter

Percival's methods were unconventional, as might be expected of a naval officer who had begun his career as a sailing master. A colleague described him as "the roughest old devil that ever was in his manners, but a kind, good hearted man at bottom." Nathaniel Hawthorne, who was to meet Percival at the Boston Navy Yard in later years, thought he saw "an eccentric expression in his face, which seemed partly wilful, partly natural. . . . He seems to have moulded and shaped himself to his own whims, till a sort of rough affectation has become thoroughly imbued throughout a kindly nature." Mad Jack's peculiar manner, coupled with his extreme sensitivity for his own and his country's honor, was to be a large factor in the events of the cruise to come.

Dolphin sailed from Chorillos, Peru, on August 18, 1825. Reaching the Mulgraves in November, she proceeded to search among the islands of the atoll, and after ten days found Cyrus Hussey and William Lay, the only survivors of the nine men left by *Globe*. The rest had been killed by the natives, who, provoked by the mutineers' flaunting of firearms and their seizure of women, massacred them with spears, stones, and hatchets. Hussey and Lay, aged twenty and eighteen respectively, were saved by native couples who wished to adopt them as sons. Neither was implicated in the mutiny. Percival took them aboard, to the great sorrow of their island parents, and after showing the flag among the islands for about a month, stood for Honolulu, where he anchored on January 14, 1826.

As *Dolphin* came up the harbor that Saturday noon, she was saluted by the guns of the fort at Honolulu and those of the ships anchored in the harbor—the American traders *Parthian*, *Convoy*, *Tamaahmaah*, *Owhyee*, *Harbinger*, and *Waverly*, and the British merchantman *Kiel*. The placid village that greeted the eyes of the sea-weary sailors was made up of about 150 thatched houses and a few buildings of frame or stone, the whole surrounded by fish ponds and taro patches. In the eastern quarter rose the unfinished stone walls of a church. But Percival soon found that this hospitable-looking place was as riddled with tensions and scandals as the New England villages he had left behind. The white residents, who numbered between one and two hundred, were divided into hostile factions engaged in a struggle for control of the government, and each faction hoped to make the visit of *Dolphin* work to its own advantage.

The first group whom Percival met were the resident merchants. They came down to greet him as he landed with First Lieutenant Hiram Paulding and Purser John Bates. The delegation was led by Dixey Wildes, partner in the Boston firm of Marshall and Wildes, and by Eliab Grimes, captain of Marshall and Wildes's brig *Owhyee*. These gentlemen escorted the American officers to their house—commonly called "the wooden house" because it was one of only two or three frame dwellings in Honolulu for an impromptu reception. After dinner Paulding and Bates visited the house of Stephen Reynolds, a testy merchant from New England, and later Bates accompanied Reynolds to a luau. No doubt the company was entertained by the hula, although Reynolds explained to the purser that the missionaries had tried to abolish it. Percival was quite soon made aware of these missionaries, who formed another of the warring factions of Oahu. They were a New England group, sent to the islands in 1820 by the American Board of Commissioners for Foreign Missions. [See "The Isles Shall Wait for His Law" in the February, 1960, AMERICAN HERITAGE.] Their self-appointed leader was Hiram Bingham, a thirty-seven-year-old Vermonter. Bingham, while doubtless sincere, had an overbearing manner and was known, even among his fellow missioners, as "Pope." What the merchants called him had best be left unsaid; one printable comment was that of Reynolds, who called him "the most impudent puppy I have seen for many a day."

Dolphin*'s captain, John "Mad Jack" Percival*

BY ETHAN ALLEN GREENWOOD; U.S. NAVAL ACADEMY MUSEUM

The American missionaries were strict Calvinists who regarded the islands as an unspoiled wilderness filled with pliable heathens waiting to be molded into a kind of utopian commonwealth. So they set out to convince the bewildered natives of their innate and hopeless depravity, and to persuade them to give up dancing and drinking in favor of prayer and meditation. Bingham soon concentrated his proselytizing efforts upon a few of the chiefs, leaving the ordinary *kanakas* to follow the example that he hoped would be set by their leaders. His principal disciples were Kalanimoku, popularly known as "Billy Pitt," and his sister, the dowager queen Kaahumanu, widow of Kamehameha I, who together acted as regents for the boy king Kauikeaouli (Kamehameha III). Both the youth's father (Kamehameha II) and his mother had died in England in 1824 while on a visit there. Billy Pitt and Kaahumanu were the two most powerful chiefs in the islands. One-eyed and dropsical, Billy Pitt was usually ill and always indolent; he acquiesced cheerfully in the missionaries' demands so long as no great effort was required of him. The haughty Kaahumanu, resistant at first, eventually became a model convert, zealous to spread the teachings of her savior—Bingham.

One of the first orders of business was the elimination of the native costume—a *pa'u* (a short skirt, usually made of tapa cloth) and a *kihei* (a kind of cape or mantle thrown loosely over the shoulders)—because it was too "revealing" by Puritan standards. While Bingham toiled with Kaahumanu over the letters of the alphabet, Mrs. Bingham and the other ladies of the mission plied their needles over the many yards of black silk needed to clothe the three-hundred-pound dowager from wrist to ankle in proper New England fashion. (All the Hawaiian chiefs at this period were large—tall, big boned, and very stout—doubtless because they had nothing to do and plenty to eat.)

So well had the missionaries succeeded in Calvinizing Oahu that when the Russian traveller Otto von Kotzebue, who had visited the islands in February, 1825, returned to Honolulu the following September, he viewed the change with horror:

The inhabitants of every house or hut in Hanaruro [Honolulu] are compelled by authority to an almost endless routine of prayers; and even the often dishonest intentions of the foreign settlers must be concealed under the veil of devotion. The streets, formerly so full of life and animation, are now deserted; games of all kinds, even the most innocent, are sternly prohibited; singing is a punishable offence; and the consummate profligacy of attempting to dance would certainly find no mercy. On Sunday, no cooking is permitted, nor must even a fire be kindled: nothing, in short, must be done; the whole day is devoted to prayer, with how much real piety may be easily imagined.

But these moralistic decrees were not the only basis for the objections of the merchants to Bingham. One of his greatest offenses in their eyes was that he tried to give the natives some idea of the proper value of trade goods so that the merchants could no longer cheat them.

On December 12, 1825, a meeting of the chiefs had been called at Honolulu to discuss Bingham's suggestion that the Decalogue be made the law of the islands. Billy Pitt and the dowager queen Kaahumanu favored the proposal; Boki, their brother and the governor of Oahu, opposed it, as did the traders, who angrily accused Bingham of trying to control the government. The proposal was shelved for the time being, but the atmosphere between merchants and missionaries was still seething when *Dolphin* dropped anchor in the roads.

On Sunday, January 15, *Dolphin* made the customary salute to the fort at Honolulu, and Percival was surprised that it was not returned. When the salute was answered

The 300-pound queen, Kaahumanu ("Feather Cloak")

on the following day, it was accompanied by an explanation that saluting on Sunday was a violation of the Sabbath. Percival began to smell a rat—or at least a missionary—in what he considered a deliberate insult to the flag of the United States. His pique was increased when on Tuesday the missionaries and their client chiefs failed to attend a party given on board *Dolphin*. The only prominent chief in attendance was Boki, who had accompanied Kamehameha II to England a few years earlier, had no illusions about the perfection of moral life in Christian countries, and had resisted Bingham's attempts to convert him, explaining that he had already been baptized in the Church of England. Boki appeared attired in the splendor of a British major general's uniform and attached himself to *Dolphin*'s officers as a friend. Most of the ship's officers established quarters ashore—Midshipmen Charles Davis and C. H. McBlair at Reynolds' house, Lieutenant William Homer, Purser Bates, and Percival himself at the wooden house of Captain Wildes. Since at this time a man could acquire a "wife" in the islands simply by casting a piece of tapa over her in the presence of witnesses, and could dismiss her at pleasure, it is not unlikely that some or all of *Dolphin*'s officers soon had "wives" on shore. Money passed hands during such liaisons, most of it apparently going to the island chiefs. The schooner was soon brought to the town dock (a hulk sunk near the fort) for repairs, and the sailors too were able to avail themselves of female companionship. All the "Dolphins" settled in for a pleasant stay at the islands.

This round of pleasure was interrupted on Friday, January 27, by the arrival of the pilot boat from Maui with news that the ship *London* of New York had been wrecked on Lanai. Since *Dolphin* had her foremast out, Percival hired the brig *Convoy*, one of Marshall and Wildes's ships, to go to the assistance of *London*.

Percival spent about a week at Lanai helping *London*'s master, Alfred P. Edwards, salvage as much as possible from the wreck. While he was away the situation at Honolulu heated up even further. Exactly what happened is not entirely clear, but it appears that a taboo on women visiting the ships in the harbor, which had been proclaimed before *Dolphin*'s arrival, began to be more strictly enforced. Several girls were imprisoned at the fort for violating the taboo, and the seamen aboard

Dolphin and the various whalers and merchant ships in the port began to find "wives" much harder to obtain except on the occasions when they received shore leave. When Percival returned to Honolulu on February 5, a delegation from the forecastle called on him to ask his assistance in having the taboo lifted. Percival promised to do what he could.

Mad Jack correctly suspected that the instigator of the taboo was Hiram Bingham. The missionaries had been delighted to learn on their arrival in the islands that the old pagan custom of taboo had been abolished. Virtually all life had been controlled by the system, and the punishment for violating it—for such an offense as letting a dog bark during a period of ritual silence—was torture and death. The missionaries had since found, however, that the taboo could be a useful tool in combating practices (including the hula) that they wished to see abolished. They viewed the sexual freedom of the natives as "lewdness," and in December Bingham had persuaded Kaahumanu that such practices should be taboo.

Up to now Mad Jack's contacts with the missionaries had been reasonably cordial, so far as they went. On January 23 Mr. Bingham had acknowledged with thanks Percival's gift of a cask of wine, and two days later Percival took morning coffee with the Binghams and another couple, who were visiting from a mission assignment at Maui. On this occasion Percival talked expansively of his voyages, and it would appear from their later remarks that the missionaries regarded him as peculiar. In any event, when he brought his men to meeting on Sunday he found himself snubbed, and he was soon grumbling to the white residents that Bingham and his friends were "a set of damned schoolmasters."

HONOLULU ACADEMY OF ARTS

Kamehameha III, *boy king of Hawaii, was painted by Robert Dampier, who visited the islands shortly before* Dolphin *arrived.*

After the sailors' complaint about the taboo against women visiting the ships, Percival remarked privately to Paulding that "the sailors would serve the missionaries right if they were to tear down their houses." Then, on February 20, a number of women were taken from their white "husbands" and put to work at carrying stone to complete the new church. One of the women was Paulding's "wife"; another was one of the Holmes girls, a white resident's half-breed daughter who was said to be Percival's "wife." This raised the captain's temper to the boiling point.

On February 22, after saluting the fort in honor of Washington's birthday, Percival went to call on the dowager queen. He had convinced himself that his honor and the honor of the United States were at stake, because *Dolphin* was being denied an indulgence that had been granted the previous year to the British frigate *Blonde.* The dialogue with Kaahumanu, conducted through an interpreter, has been variously reported. Something like the following seems to have taken place:

Percival: "Who governs the Islands?"

Kaahumanu: "The young king."

Percival: "And who governs him?"

Kaahumanu: "I do."

Percival: "And who governs you?"

Kaahumanu (piously): "My God."

Percival (pointing a finger scornfully): "You lie, you damned old bitch! Mr. Bingham governs you!"

Percival also told Kaahumanu, apparently as a bluff: "Take heed. My people will come: if the women are not forthcoming they will not obey my word. . . . By and by they will come to get women, and if they do not obtain them, they will fight, and my vessel is just like fire."

This simmering pot came to a boil at last on the morning of Sunday, February 26, when Percival boarded *Dolphin* for a muster. Several men who had caused trouble on shore the previous Sunday were again requesting liberty, but he ordered them to remain on board. Liberty was granted to the usual number of seamen—about twenty-seven, perhaps a third of the ship's company—and Percival admonished them to go to meeting, stay sober, and return on board promptly.

But the dozen or more grog shops of Honolulu were hospitable, and in the course of the afternoon some of *Dolphin*'s men paid them extended visits. There they

PEABODY MUSEUM, SALEM, MASS.

Merchantmen and whalers found Honolulu a most pleasant port-of-call. C. E. Bensell, who visited the city in 1821, painted this view.

found sailors from the whaling ships, and the two groups commiserated with one another on their troubles with the missionaries. The discussion waxed hot, and presently several of the whalemen and a number of "Dolphins" picked up clubs and set off for the Mission House.

On the way there they passed the new house of Billy Pitt, a substantial stone structure with a forty-foot verandah across its front. The rioters stopped long enough to smash the verandah windows and frighten a group assembling upstairs for evening worship. Bingham had left the house ahead of the mob and raced home by a back way, but finding that his wife had prudently locked the door, he returned to Billy Pitt's yard, with the rioters now on his heels. The native converts, seeing Bingham surrounded by the seamen, intervened, and there was a small scuffle from which Bingham escaped and returned to his house. This time Mrs. Bingham let him in.

Just then Percival, with two of *Dolphin*'s midshipmen, McBlair and Schermerhorn, rushed into the yard, roaring "I'll teach you to disgrace us!" and laying about him with his cane. With the help of the natives the officers seized and bound every sailor in sight and sent them on board *Dolphin*. Two of the men carried off a third, who had been knocked out by a club. Bingham leaned out of a window and shouted that the clubbed seaman had been killed (for so it appeared, although the man did not die) by another of the sailors, and not by a native. "I wish they were all killed," Percival retorted.

When the men had been secured and the excitement had passed, Percival returned to call on Bingham. He assured the missionary that the damage caused by the rioters would be repaired but pointed out that the decree against shipboard fraternization was the source of the trouble. He reminded Bingham that prostitution was common enough in America and England and accused him of interfering with the government of the islands by putting forth the Decalogue as law. Bingham denied it, but Percival said, "You are going on too fast; you will have a terrible reaction shortly. . . . The tabu must come off. I will not leave the islands until it is taken off; I would rather have my hands tied or even cut off and be carried home maimed as a criminal than to have it said that Lord Byron [captain of the *Blonde*] was allowed a privilege greater than was allowed me."

Next morning Bingham, at Percival's invitation, boarded *Dolphin* to help single out the rioters for punishment. He declined, however, to witness the flogging, saying as he went over the side, "I hope they lay it on well."

From that day until *Dolphin* sailed, none of her seamen was allowed on shore. But within a few days the nervous Governor Boki lifted the taboo for the duration of her stay. Meanwhile, as a result of the rioting, Percival on March 3 sent a letter to other commanders in the port:

The excitement of the Seamen towards Mr. Bingham who is at the head of the Missionaries at this Island is such, and from the recent outrage committed by them from the belief he has interfered with some of the Civil regulations of this place, and thereby deprived them of an enjoyment they have always been in the participation of, when they visit this Island: I have to request you will let but a small proportion of your Crew come on shore on Sunday. By complying with this request you will aid my wishes in preventing anxiety to the Missionary family.

Bingham, however, while he may have felt less anxious, contrived to take umbrage at the letter, inferring that the "enjoyment" mentioned by Percival could mean only one thing. He spent a good part of the next several months in preparing charges against *Dolphin*'s commander, to be forwarded to the American Board of Commissioners for Foreign Missions. These, together with charges brought by Edwards, ex-captain of *London*, were to cause considerable trouble for Percival on his return to the United States.

For Percival was also engaged in a quarrel with Edwards, which began to wax hotter just as his imbroglio with the missionaries seemed to be cooling off. A sharp character, Edwards had been transporting a large amount of uninsured specie aboard *London;* he hoped, by concealing its presence from his underwriters, to avoid paying the portion of the salvage charges that should have accrued to it. Percival, who had taken charge of the specie as a favor to him, got wind of this and refused to relinquish the money until a written accounting of it had been made, and until the bill for charter of *Convoy* ($815) had been paid.

While this matter was still being argued, Edwards made arrangements to charter the native-owned brig *Becket* to take himself and crew, his remaining cargo, and the specie to China. Percival was called upon to witness the charter, but upon reading it he discovered that it had been drawn in such a way that the United States was made guarantor of payment. Accordingly, he declined to witness the document. Edwards snapped that he had merely come for Percival's signature and not to discuss the terms of the charter. This sneer lit the fuse to the Percival temper. Mad Jack called Edwards a few choice names, among the mildest of which were "liar" and "scoundrel," and then collared him and threatened to throw him over a balustrade. CONTINUED ON PAGE 85

BERNICE P. BISHOP MUSEUM, HONOLULU

Kalanimoku (Billy Pitt), at the time minister to Kamehameha II, *wore European garb to be baptized as a Roman Catholic in 1819 aboard the French exploration ship* L'Uranie. *The quarter-deck was rather strangely decorated with flags for the occasion, most improperly in the case of the Stars and Stripes. Jacques Arago, the expedition's draftsman, who painted the ceremony, recalled that several of the king's wives preferred to sit on the deck. Later, Protestant missionaries accepted Billy Pitt's baptism as valid, and he took communion in their church.*

THE
PAPER
TRUST

By BERNARD A. WEISBERGER

To begin with, the Presidential libraries do not look like what they are. Each one is, in fact, a miniature Office of Public Records. And scholars who frequent such offices know that they are found in capital cities, in buildings that are heavy, ornamented, slowly discoloring monuments to bureaucrats dead and gone. The National Archives of the United States—America's public records—are, to give one example, housed in an oversized Greek temple near the intersection of Constitution and Pennsylvania avenues in Washington, D.C.

But the six libraries for Presidential papers, which are administered by the National Archives and Records Service (NARS) of the General Services Administration, are something else. The Herbert Hoover Library modestly hugs the flat ground of West Branch, Iowa, calculatedly as unpretentious as Hoover's nearby birthplace or the well-preserved blacksmith shop of his father, where he learned by observation the value of hard work and austerity. Franklin D. Roosevelt's is in a building that blends neatly into the surroundings of a Hudson River gentleman's estate at Hyde Park, New York. Harry S. Truman's spreads itself on a grassy knoll not far from an expressway in Independence, Missouri, once the gateway to the limitless West, now a suburb of Kansas City. A tendency toward expansion becomes visible in Abilene, Kansas. There, in the Eisenhower Center, a library of Kansas limestone and imported marble faces a museum across an open court, flanked by a Place of Meditation (the word *chapel* being carefully avoided) and a set of monumental pylons presented by the Kansas Daughters of the American Revolution and the Soroptomist Clubs of Kansas. On the campus of the University of Texas at Austin a rectangular, flat-capped tower of pinkish travertine rises from what landscaping will turn into a spacious plaza. To be opened in May, 1971, it will contain the Lyndon B. Johnson Library; an adjoining, lower structure will house the Lyndon B. Johnson School of Public Affairs. Both are the architectural creation of Skidmore, Owings & Merrill, the firm that has designed many of the steel-and-glass temples of industry on New York's Park Avenue. Fiscal and other uncertainties have delayed the construction of the John F. Kennedy Library, but eventually an oval-shaped cluster of buildings and malls in Cambridge, Massachusetts, will contain the library itself, the Harvard-affiliated Kennedy School of Government, and possibly a third "related facilities" building.

These are a long way from the attics in which Presidents of a simpler day stored their papers; the contents of these libraries, too, are of a magnitude and complexity that stretch the imagination. First of all, there are the actual papers of the Executive Office—row on row, shelf after shelf, of the memoranda, letters, reports, studies, schedules, briefs, minutes, tables, abstracts, lists, projections, drafts, forms, authorizations, and all the infinite variety of documents through which Executive power somewhat soggily asserts itself. Next, there are the truly personal papers—the records of the human beings who briefly occupied the White House and of many members of their administrations. These comprise an incredible miscellany of mail, including thousands of letters from ordinary citizens who reach out to touch the majesty of office in revealing notes that beg, cajole, flatter, and often obscenely condemn the President. In addition there are clippings, photographs, tape recordings, reprints, motion-picture films, sketches, and such minor social records as greetings, invitations, acknowledgments, and farewells. Finally, there is a third category of material, housed in the museum that is part of each Presidential library—the objects accumulated by a President in office: paintings of (and sometimes by) the Chief Executive, statuettes, stamps, ship models, miniature weapons and vehicles, fishing tackle, stuffed animals, dishes, silverware, mugs and goblets, clothing for the First Lady, toys for the First Children, souvenirs of historic occasions, books, cartoons, prints and musical scores autographed by their creators, rugs, tapestries, plaques—the gifts of ordinary citizens and heads of state alike to the representative of the American people.

The new Presidential libraries raise a question: Can the documentary grain be separated from the documentary chaff?

These unscholarly items have, in some cases, achieved a kind of immortality in their own right—the collar of Roosevelt's famous Scottie, Fala; the sign on Truman's desk, THE BUCK STOPS HERE; John Kennedy's rocking chair. They are the items that, when displayed, bring in the tourists by thousands. While the historians, sitting shirt-sleeved in the research rooms and peering quizzically at the documents, may take little interest in the public thronging through the museum displays, the directors of the libraries do not scorn the sightseers. They reason that among the crowds of children in Snoopy T-shirts, Sears jeans, and Keds sneakers, smelling of Howard Johnson's peppermint gum and Good and Plenty licorice, peering at the cases through Rexall sunglasses, there may be future Morisons and Schlesingers. (The tourists and the researchers do not see each other, but in the Johnson Library the sightseers will be able to see what the archivists are working on. The architect has made the stacks visible from the museum through a glass wall and has decreed that the papers be kept in eye-catching scarlet boxes.)

The libraries are the creations of an unusual collaboration. Each has been

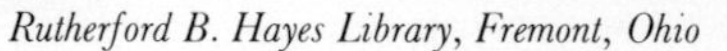

Rutherford B. Hayes Library, Fremont, Ohio

Herbert Hoover Memorial Library, West Branch, Iowa

Franklin D. Roosevelt Library, Hyde Park, New York

built by private subscription among the friends of a President (except for the Johnson Library, which Texas will pay for and own as part of its state university campus). The President so honored, on his retirement, deposits his papers in the library, and both building and contents become a gift to the people of the United States. The federal government then puts archivists to work in the role of white-collar monks, guarding the precious manuscripts against the ravages of time, weather, chance, and desperate men.

With each succeeding Presidency the sheer volume of material has increased. It is estimated that George Washington wrote perhaps twenty-five thousand letters all told. By Franklin Roosevelt's time the President's own letters, plus the other documents he had collected during his public life, were measured in the linear feet of space they occupied when boxed and shelved. The total was nearly 2,500 feet—almost half a mile of such records. The Roosevelt Library did not confine itself simply to preserving the papers taken from the White House after Roosevelt's death. Like the Presidential libraries that followed, it sought and accepted the manuscripts of the President's co-workers and associates throughout his career in government. As a result the Roosevelt Library now has over twenty-one million pages of manuscript on paper, after a quarter-century of growth. But the Kennedy Library, not yet open in its permanent quarters, already has more than seventeen million pages on paper, plus two and a half million on microfilm, representing an administration that lasted less than three years—in addition to a million and a half feet of motion-picture film and more than fifteen hundred sound recordings (both discs and tapes). The Johnson Library has thirty million pages on paper, 5,500,000 on microfilm, half a million photographs (compared to 93,052 in the Roosevelt Library, the nearest competitor in this field), 2,010,420 feet of motion-picture film, and 3,025 sound recordings for the ears of the future.

It is estimated that President Nixon's records, even if he were to serve but one term, will exceed Johnson's in volume. What the cost of a Nixon Library (already in the planning stages) will be is uncertain, but since the Roosevelt Library cost $367,000 to build, as against the several millions that the John F. Kennedy Library will require, it may be guessed that the amount will not be small. The expense of maintaining the six institutions—including the two not yet complete—in fiscal 1970 was approximately 1.8 million dollars in appropriated funds, which allowed for a personnel of 146. Certainly it seems a modest sum, nowadays, to care for donated buildings and lands worth many millions, and for papers whose value to history is presumed to be incalculable.

But are the treasures of the Presidential libraries actually priceless? There are some who doubt it, who fear that, if only because of their stupefying massiveness, the Presidential papers will not yield up the shape of the past to future historians in the way that fossil bones deliver the outlines of prehistoric giant lizards to knowledgeable paleontologists. Scattered widely over the country, some argue, the libraries will be visited only by pilgrims who are seeking the relics in the museums and by a handful of scholars who appear seasonally like wildfowl (at every academic vacation) to scrabble for the materials of dissertations. Will the Presidential libraries, in fact, become—in Columbia historian Henry Graff's speculative phrase—the pyramids of our time? Or will they, as their staffs hope, help in the critical task of preserving the nation's records so that it may learn wisdom by a searching look at all its yesterdays?

To answer that question demands a review of the nature and history of Presidential papers and a survey of the current limitations on their use. The picture is sometimes discouraging. To begin with, a skeptical American may be pardoned if he believes that gratitude is uncalled-for when a President makes a "gift" of

Harry S. Truman Library, Independence, Missouri

Dwight D. Eisenhower Center,

his papers to the public. Why should the people be thankful, he reasons, for being given what is theirs in the first place? For is it not true that the President's correspondence is a part of the official record of the government? And does it not therefore belong to the taxpayers fully as much as anything else created or purchased with government monies?

Astonishingly, the answer is No. Ordinary civil servants—even Cabinet members—are obliged by law to keep account of their doings, and in so doing to create the fallout of official documents that keeps archivists in prosperity. They may not destroy or remove whatever may be needful for a competent authority later to review their public performance. But the President of the United States is himself an independent government agency. In a sense he is accountable only to God, the Constitution, and the electorate. What comes into his office during his tenure is his alone.

George Washington, who set so many Presidential precedents, simply took his papers—including all the written matter he had exchanged with members of his official family—back to Mount Vernon with him, presumably to nestle alongside his old plantation account books, and no one was disposed to challenge him. John Adams followed suit because, according to one scholar, he did not want his then-hated successor, Thomas Jefferson, nosing among his letters. When Jefferson himself did the same in 1809, the precedent had hardened. It was not challenged until 1886, when the Senate made bold to ask for certain papers belonging to Grover Cleveland, which were then not even in the White House but on file in the office of the Attorney General. Cleveland characteristically rapped the Senate's knuckles. "I regard the papers and documents . . . intended for my use and action," he wrote, "purely unofficial and private, not infrequently confidential, and having reference to the performance of a duty exclusively mine. . . . I suppose if I desired to take them into my custody I might do so with entire propriety, and if I saw fit to destroy them no one could complain. . . ." The senators did not press the matter further.

Presidents came and went. They took their papers with them and did things to make archivists shudder. The precious documents were dumped in attics; rummaged by heirs for autographs and souvenirs to bestow on friends; winnowed of "improper" material by worshipful widows, executors, and official biographers; and scrawled on by playful children. Some were burnt by accident—many of Andrew Jackson's, for example—and some perished in flames by design, like those of Millard Fillmore (by the deathbed command of his son) and, reputedly, those of Martin Van Buren and Ulysses Grant, who were either indifferent to, or wary of, the curiosity of posterity.

Some, of course, were sold to libraries (often by heirs in need of cash) whose directors sensed the vital importance of the neglected records to historical research. The Library of Congress worked hard at getting a complete Presidential collection and up to 1940 had spent $170,000 in purchases of ex-Presidents' papers. Universities and state and local historical societies acquired fragments of individual Presidents' papers.

There were shining exceptions. The family of Rutherford B. Hayes presented his carefully kept papers, as well as the family estate, to the state of Ohio, which built a memorial library on the site. Opened in 1916, it has since become an important center for the study of the Reconstruction era. The bulk of the papers of the Presidents from James A. Garfield through Calvin Coolidge—with the exception of Warren Harding, whose papers are at the Ohio Historical Society, in Columbus—were given to the Library of Congress. Herbert Hoover deposited his in a special library, now known as the Hoover Institution on War, Revolution and Peace, on the campus of Stanford University; there they joined the materials he had accumulated in a world-ranging career as engineer and famine relief administrator (but as it turned out later, they did not stay there). When Franklin Roosevelt began to think about leaving the White House, he might have followed what has been called the Library of Congress model. But he regarded himself as having a special problem, and, characteristically, he looked for a precedent-breaking way to solve it.

In February, 1938, Roosevelt wrote to his fellow sailing enthusiast and Harvard alumnus Samuel Eliot Morison, asking for advice on the "somewhat ambitious thought" of creating a repository for materials "relating to this period of our national history." Without a special effort they would be scattered throughout libraries and collections across the entire country. "For example," Roosevelt noted, "my own papers should, under the old method, be divided among the Navy Department, the Library of Congress, the New York State Historical Division in Albany, the New York City Historical Society, Harvard University, and various members of my family." Morison quickly replied. He thought that a separate New Deal archive would not be a good idea. But the President's own papers might well be kept together somewhere—it did not matter where,

CONTINUED ON PAGE 104

Abilene, Kansas

Temporary John F. Kennedy Library, Waltham, Massachusetts

Lyndon Baines Johnson Library, Austin, Texas

PHOTOS COURTESY OF LIBRARIES CONCERNED, EXCEPT KENNEDY: *New York Times*

NKEL

UPI

AMERICAN HERITAGE BOOK SELECTION

HOW *NOT* TO FLY THE ATLANTIC

By RICHARD MONTAGUE

On May 20, 1927, when Charles A. Lindbergh took off on his famous solo flight, he was only one of several aspirants for the title of first man to fly an airplane nonstop between New York and Paris. Five men had already died attempting the feat. Two more planes were preparing to take off. For some weeks, Roosevelt Field on Long Island had been swarming with fliers, backers, and mechanics nursing, testing, and perfecting the planes that would attempt the unprecedented flight. Prize money had been put up, and the press had whooped up excitement about the contest in daily bulletins flashed all over the world. Commander Richard Evelyn Byrd, already famous for his North Pole flight, was the leader of one of the crews primed to go. Another interested party was Charles A. Levine, a slightly shady millionaire and promoter. Levine, whose initials, by coincidence, were the same as Lindbergh's—one of the very few similarities between the two men—had in the tense weeks of waiting at Roosevelt Field managed to antagonize several prospective pilots and his plane's designer by shabby financial dealings and his general arrogance and bombast.

As everyone knows, Lindbergh made it, landing in Paris on the following night. Less well-known is what happened next at Roosevelt Field. In his forthcoming book, Oceans, Poles and Airmen, *from which this excerpt is taken, Richard Montague tells of the second "successful" nonstop transatlantic flight. The book will be published this month by Random House, Inc.*

Lindbergh's spectacular flight, which brought him world fame overnight, did not dampen the enthusiasm of his rivals. For the aviators he had left behind at Roosevelt Field there seemed to be several additional aerial goals whose attainment would make them heroes in their turn.

All these people staring skyward are waiting at the Berlin airport for the official *welcome of the* Columbia, *after its nonstop flight to Germany. The fliers had trouble finding Berlin.*

Charles A. Levine's Bellanca, the plane that held the endurance record, probably could fly farther than Lindbergh's Ryan and might be used for a trip to Berlin, Rome, or Vienna. And Commander Byrd's three-engined Fokker could symbolize the big, safe airliners of the future, thus advancing the cause of aeronautic science.

Levine had the last word of the legend *New York→Paris* on the side of his plane painted out. The machine still was going to fly to Europe, he said, but he refused to specify where or when.

Grover Whalen, vice president of the company that was backing Byrd, declared that Lindbergh's triumph had failed to demonstrate that ocean flying was safe. He contrasted the trimotor Fokker with the single-engined Ryan and announced that the principal goals sought by his company, which was headed by department-store magnate Lewis Rodman Wanamaker, had not been achieved by the *Spirit of St. Louis*. It appeared that Mr. Wanamaker's aim of advancing the cause of aeronautic science had numerous important ramifications. Many things of great value, said Whalen, remained for Commander Byrd to prove.

Four days after Lindbergh landed in Paris, James Dole, the Hawaiian pineapple king, came up with some prize offers of his own. He announced a first prize of twenty-five thousand dollars and a second of ten thousand for the first nonstop flights from America's Pacific Coast to his island Elysium. He invited Lindbergh to enter the contest any time during the next year.

Levine promptly announced that his plane, the *Columbia*, might go after the money. In the meantime, he said, it might fly nonstop to Rome. On June 2 he had

UPI

Sandwiched between wing-collared officials, the two American fliers pose for a news photo shortly after their arrival in Berlin—Clarence Chamberlin in the knickers favored by sportsmen of the era, Charles Levine in his impromptu flying suit.

Clarence Chamberlin, his pilot, take him up in a climbing test in which they reached an altitude of nine thousand feet. During this and other flights Levine, who had already had a few flying lessons, took over the controls to familiarize himself with the plane's performance.

Rumors were spreading that the *Columbia* was about to start for Germany. These were denied by Levine, but shortly after midnight of June 4 Chamberlin announced he would take off in a few hours. He refused to name his destination, but at the hangar he received a radiogram from Lincoln Eyre, Berlin correspondent of the *New York Times*, saying that all Germany was awaiting the *Columbia*'s arrival. Chamberlin grinned. "Well, we'll be glad to drop in on them on the way back," he said, leaving reporters with the impression that he hoped to fly even farther. He did say he would keep the plane in the air as long as its engine functioned and its fuel held out.

He gave the Nassau County police the required take-off notice, and a squad of motorcycle police escorted the *Columbia* as it was towed tail first from its hangar at the adjacent Curtiss Field to the Roosevelt Field runway. The police also kept a small crowd at bay while mechanics loaded the main gas tank with 390 gallons and put aboard the plane fifty-five additional gallons in five-gallon cans.

Who, if anybody, was going along with Chamberlin? When reporters asked the airman, he only smiled. Nobody paid much attention to a black limousine when it rolled up near the starting area at the western end of the runway. The vehicle contained Mr. and Mrs. Levine, but they had come, it was assumed, merely to see the *Columbia* take off.

Levine, in a pinstriped blue business suit and without a hat for his balding head, got out of the car with a roll of charts. He walked over to the plane and thrust the charts through the window. "Are you going?" somebody asked him. Levine merely looked at the questioner. Somebody else inquired who was going to be navigator. "He's not here yet," Levine replied. A few minutes later he disappeared in the crowd.

Harold Kinkaid asked that the engine be started. Kinkaid, known generally as Doc, was a Wright engine man who had accompanied Byrd on his North Pole flight and had tuned up Lindbergh's engine. Now he listened with an expert ear to the roar of another Whirlwind engine. "Never heard a motor sound better," he said. A mechanic shut it off.

Another mechanic discovered that the main gas tank would hold ten more gallons. These were poured in to make a total of 455, five more than Lindbergh had carried. Then John Carisi, a mechanic who had worked on the plane devotedly for months, started the engine again. Although he had often declared that he was not "one of those emotional Wops," he was so overcome by the apparent certainty that the *Columbia* was really going at last that he climbed up to the window and planted a resounding kiss on Chamberlin's cheek.

Chamberlin idled the engine for a few minutes and then opened it up. Its roar resounded down the field, and the plane trembled and strained against the wheel chocks. Then Chamberlin throttled it down again, looked at a knot of persons behind the ropes, and nodded. And suddenly out of the knot darted Levine. Keeping his head down and looking at nobody, he ran to the plane on the side opposite Chamberlin, opened the door, and climbed in. Quickly he closed the door and slumped down in his seat, keeping his gaze averted from his wife.

Grace Levine had once been known as the Belle of Williamsburg, for she had won two beauty contests in that section of Brooklyn. She had been a good wife to Levine, had borne him two children, and had stood by him in the face of criticism and ridicule. She and her husband had discussed recent rumors that he might fly to Europe with Chamberlin, and together they had laughed at their absurdity. Once she had said she would burn the plane if he attempted to fly across the ocean in it.

Now she turned to some friends who had come with her to see the takeoff. "What's all this foolishness of Charles getting into the plane?" she asked. Nobody knew, and she became frightened and started to get out of the car.

Carisi ran up to reassure her. "It's all right," he said. "It's only a test run." And indeed for a while it seemed to be only that. When the wheel chocks were removed, Chamberlin gunned the plane down the runway for several hundred yards. Then, to avoid hitting some people who had pressed in too close to the takeoff strip, he turned off the course and returned to the starting area near Curtiss Field.

Carisi sprinted over to the machine and stood beside the window, one foot on a wheel. "What are you doing, Mr. Levine?" he yelled. "Your wife is going out of her mind! She has got the idea that you are going to Europe in the plane!"

But Grace Levine was now smiling happily. Her husband wasn't going to fly after all. She laughed at her former nervousness. How foolish she had been! She was still laughing when Chamberlin opened up the engine again. The propeller blast blew Carisi away, and the *Columbia* started to roll.

Now the monoplane was roaring over the same strip Lindbergh had used, a runway that was dry instead of soggy. With six inches more of wingspread—46½ feet—and some five hundred pounds more load than the *Spirit of St. Louis* had carried, it took off in two thousand feet, about half the distance its rival had covered.

It was a beautiful Saturday morning. The sun was a glowing red ball, and the little clouds above it were edged with gold. But Grace Levine was sobbing hysterically as the small monoplane climbed into the air shortly after six o'clock. "He isn't really going!" she cried. "He isn't really going!" And then, as the plane became a dot and disappeared, she began to weep bitterly.

The faithful Carisi came over and put his arms around her. "He'll make it," he told her. "You should be proud of him. He's a brave boy."

Only a few people beside Chamberlin knew that Levine had planned to go. Giuseppe Bellanca, the plane's designer, had suspected it and opposed the plan because he felt that Chamberlin needed a competent navigator. Still another who had had an inkling of Levine's intention was Samuel Hartman, his attorney.

Hartman told reporters later that Levine sat up most of the night before the takeoff writing notes to his wife and his lawyer and making a will disposing of an estate of five million dollars. The note to Hartman said: "Well, I'm off. Bet you'll be surprised, but don't worry. We will make it. Will cable you first moment I can and wish you would sail over to join me when I dine with Mussolini."

In spite of his reputation Levine had shown courage in attempting a transatlantic flight, and many assumed he must be a good fellow after all. There was talk that whatever his faults, he had vindicated himself. Now that he was at least temporarily famous, people wanted to believe in his essential nobility, an attribute they had already accorded to Lindbergh.

The *Columbia*'s takeoff made big headlines both in the United States and Europe, even though the plane's destination was uncertain. Its two most likely objectives seemed to be Berlin and Rome, though there also was

UPI

Several days later, the fliers' wives arrived in Germany by ship. The heroes were on hand to greet them. Grace Levine, recovered from the shock of Charles's precipitant trip, looks blooming, and Mrs. Chamberlin gives her husband a well-deserved kiss.

speculation about Warsaw, Vienna, and Prague.

The German capital prepared for a welcome that would outdo Paris' greeting to Lindbergh. High government officials, it was said, would meet the gallant fliers at Tempelhof Airport, where three thousand police would keep the immense crowd from storming the little monoplane. The Berlin field and other airports at Cologne, Hamburg, and Bremen would be kept lighted through the night. And Lufthansa, the German air trust, would send out planes to fly along the western border to meet the *Columbia* and escort it in.

Newspapers ran off extras about the flight, and hotels set up information bureaus to provide excited guests with the latest news on the plane's progress. Attention centered on Chamberlin rather than on Levine, who was then known to few Europeans. It was considered a happy omen that the last two syllables of the pilot's name spelled the name of the city toward which the Bellanca seemed to be headed.

But Rome saw itself, not Berlin, as the fliers' goal. After all, for a plane designed by an Italian what could be a more appropriate destination than the Eternal City? Italian newspaper presses whirled out extra after extra, and crowds collected in front of the newspaper offices to get the latest bulletins.

Aboard the machine all was not entirely well. After the first hundred miles Chamberlin noticed that the earth inductor compass was misbehaving. He was attempting to follow a great-circle course modified in accordance with last-minute weather forecasts. Setting the indicator to match his course, he tried to keep the pointer at zero. But the pointer wouldn't stay steady. At Newport, Rhode Island, they were four or five miles off course. And when they reached what appeared to be Cape Cod, the needle began swinging from side to side in a meaningless and maddening dance. Moreover, there seemed to be an extra hook on the arm of land below that didn't appear on their chart. They couldn't be sure they were really over the Cape.

Chamberlin circled about, hoping that the aberrant compass would return to normal. They had come about two hundred miles and had thirty-four hundred to go. Should they rely on their fifty-dollar magnetic compass? Or should they fly back to Roosevelt Field and have the thousand-dollar earth inductor compass adjusted? They talked it over and decided to go on.

Chamberlin kept circling till he got a bearing on what he thought was the tip of Cape Cod and had oriented himself with the help of the sun. Then, steering by the magnetic compass, which was jiggling from the engine vibration, he headed out over the water toward Nova Scotia. The air was smooth, and they flew along a few hundred feet over the ocean, sighting several sailing yachts and fishing smacks and waving to their crews. But a northeast wind was rising to slow them down.

In two hours, Chamberlin figured, they ought to hit Yarmouth, Nova Scotia. But the second hour passed with only blue water below. A third hour faded into the past. What if the magnetic compass had also failed and was prompting them to fly in circles on a crazy course that would end in a splash and a hiss and then silence?

The main gas tank was shaped like an upright piano, and the eleven 5-gallon cans were strapped on its shelf. Levine now emptied the first of these into the tank and then jettisoned it to clear the space on the tank shelf and give access to the back part of the cabin.

Finally, to their relief, they sighted Nova Scotia. Their magnetic compass was working properly after all. Chamberlin took the new bearing his charts called for and pointed the *Columbia*'s nose for Newfoundland. The wind had now veered from dead ahead to quartering from the east and southeast. To counteract its thrust Chamberlin had to crab sideways into the wind.

By the time they reached Halifax, the wind was blowing across their course from the south, necessitating more crabbing and slowing their progress eastward by about thirty miles an hour. They were now two hours behind schedule because of the winds, but the air currents were shifting at last in their favor and starting to push the plane along. Things began to look up.

Chamberlin climbed to two thousand feet to let the plane take advantage of the tail wind and headed for Trepassey, Newfoundland. He had decided to go slightly south of the great-circle route to avoid a storm area shown on their weather map. By the time they reached Trepassey, Levine had emptied and thrown out the last of the five-gallon gas cans, and the way to the rear of the cabin was open. Chamberlin let his companion take over the plane and went back to put on his cold weather clothing—heavy woolen drawers to be pulled over his trousers and a woolen shirt with a parka hood. Then he stretched out on the shelf of the gas tank to get a little rest. But he couldn't sleep.

Some twenty-five hundred feet below them stretched the last of Newfoundland they would see—rough, desolate country blotched with swamps and wasteland. After a while they sighted the ocean and, a few miles offshore, what seemed to be the white sail of a fishing boat.

The red sun was sliding down behind the world to the west, and its last rays picked out the white triangle and turned it a luminous pink. It was like a great jewel risen from the blue of the sea. Then they realized it was an iceberg. Chamberlin took a final bearing and headed east across the Atlantic. Levine grinned. "Europe next stop," he said. "Well, here goes nothing."

They flew on toward the night that was creeping over the northern sea. Soon they were looking down on a whole spattering of icebergs. While admiring their beauty, Chamberlin used them to check the plane's drift till they faded like ghosts into the darkness.

The air was now so calm that the remarkably stable Bellanca was flying itself without the touch of human hand or foot. Chamberlin had attached to the rudder bar a spring he had devised to compensate for propeller torque, and left the controls alone for as much as two hundred miles at a stretch.

Presently they were soaring above clouds. And then, through a rift, they saw the lights of a ship three or four thousand feet down. Levine blinked a flashlight, but the boat gave no answering signal. The incident depressed them. They wanted to be sighted and reported often.

After an hour or so they saw the lights of another ship; this one instantly answered Levine's flashlight blinkings. Immensely cheered, they flew on. Only later did they learn that no report from either vessel was ever received on shore.

Soon clouds blanketed the world below, and then the gray mass started up toward them. The Bellanca climbed till it could climb no more. With its still-heavy load of gasoline it couldn't struggle higher than fifteen thousand feet, and the cloud bank ahead of it loomed three or four thousand feet higher.

The short northern night was fading ahead of them and giving way to a slow dawn. In this meager light the plane entered the gray mist. The temperature was one degree below freezing. A thin layer of ice began to form on the cabin windshield and on the leading edges of the wings.

Wing ice was a terror to the fliers of those days. They had no equipment to melt it or break it up. And many planes crashed because the thin film changed the contours and destroyed the lifting effectiveness of wings, as well as adding to the load the machine was carrying. So Chamberlin cut the throttle and headed down through the blankness, hoping for a space between the underside of the cloud bank and the sea. He also hoped that the altimeter would continue to work. A faulty reading could plunge them into the waves.

Ten thousand feet. Six thousand. Three thousand. Two. Still nothing visible below but gray. One thousand. Chamberlin flattened out a little. He would ease the plane down to a hundred feet but no farther. Then he would level off and perhaps leave the mist behind.

He had been revving up the engine at intervals to keep the sparkplugs free of oil so that the Whirlwind would be ready to use when he needed it. And suddenly he did need it. Below eight hundred feet the gray ghostly stuff thinned, and whitecaps appeared. There was enough light now to see that it was raining.

Apparently this was the storm area shown on their weather map. They could run out of it, they had been told, by turning south. Chamberlin banked to the right, but for an hour the rain continued to beat against the windshield. Then they emerged into clear weather.

The water had a brown appearance, and the air was so warm that both men discarded their heavy clothing. Chamberlin decided they were over the Gulf Stream and coursing the steamer lanes to Europe. He set a new great-circle course for Land's End.

Their watches were still running on New York time, five hours later than London's. So when the sun appeared out of the sea, they did some quick figuring. This sunrise was two and a half hours earlier than the June 5th sunrise scheduled for New York. Hurrah! They must be half way across the ocean.

The wind was still behind them, and the Bellanca was moving toward Europe at a speed they estimated as about 120 miles an hour. The magnetic compass, as far as they could tell from the position of the sun, was still giving accurate guidance. They celebrated with a Sunday breakfast of oranges, chicken soup, and coffee.

About nine o'clock they sighted a Scandinavian tramp and circled the ship. The crew waved. The fliers felt sure that the ship would report them—and learned later that she didn't.

But at four thirty that afternoon they got one of the big thrills of the trip. The liner *Mauretania* appeared so suddenly and so close that it seemed as if she had sprung out of the sea. The big Cunarder, with her four red funnels, white superstructure, and black hull, and with flags flying and decks lined with passengers, was a glorious sight. Chamberlin pointed the plane down toward her and flashed by at the height of her top deck. Then he banked sharply and came up on the opposite side.

Throttling the plane, he kept just abreast of the liner, while her wildly excited passengers tossed hats, books, and umbrellas into the air. They had read about the *Columbia*'s takeoff in the ship's news bulletins and could readily identify it.

As they flew along abreast of the liner, Levine noticed a group of officers on the bridge. He leaned out the window and made motions with his hands as if he were punching a telegraph key. The officers nodded, and the *Mauretania* did what was asked, giving the United States the first news that the plane was nearing Europe.

Levine leafed through a copy of the *New York Times* that they had aboard. Its marine page told them that the liner had left Southhampton at noon the day before. Then he looked again at the chart. It showed the lanes that transatlantic liners were using that June. From this data they calculated they were four or five hundred miles west of Land's End (actually the distance was about 350) and pretty well on course.

Then Chamberlin opened the throttle, pulled ahead of

CONTINUED ON PAGE 80

THE CIVIL WAR AS ROMANCE

# of Noble Warriors and MAIDENS CHASTE

Oriana Weems, Alma Lamour, Caroline Fitzhugh, Seth Rawbon, Netley Shiplake, Mordaunt—none of these improbable names is likely to mean anything to the modern reader, but to the generation that lived through the Civil War, and sighed and wept over the novels that it spawned, the names were as familiar as Scarlett O'Hara is to us. For these are some of the heroes and heroines of a genre of Civil War romance that flooded the market almost as soon as the shooting started.

If one sets out today to read these novels, he needs to be a rummager in the musty attics of literature and a bit of a masochist as well. Except for a few books of lasting importance, most notably John William De Forest's *Miss Ravenel's Conversion from Secession to Loyalty* and Stephen Crane's *Red Badge of Courage*, many of these novels are so bad that there can be only one reason (aside from camp) for rescuing them, even temporarily, from the obscurity in which they so deservedly rest: these popular books reveal much about reading tastes of the period and attitudes toward the war.

The most avid readers of popular fiction during the late nineteenth century were women, and from their ranks came those female writers the likes of whom had earlier provoked Nathaniel Hawthorne to make his disgruntled comment about "that horde of damned female scribblers." In all justice, Hawthorne should have levelled his blast at scribbling men, too, for they equalled and sometimes surpassed the women at concocting labyrinthine plots and absurdly unrealistic characters.

That the spirit of flowery romance was not limited to Civil War novelists is proved by this 1865 painting by George Lambdin. His scene of belle-kissing-sword is called The Consecration.

BERRY-HILL GALLERIES, INC., NEW YORK

These novelists seldom bothered the brains of their readers by paying any serious attention to such vital issues of the war as slavery, industrialism versus agrarianism, and the conflict between states' rights and federal power. Above all, they were generally careful not to shock delicate feminine sensibilities by requiring readers to look too closely at any blood or physical pain. In many of the novels the war is the stage where thrilling dramas of heroism unfold. Battle scenes enable the writer to display the unflinching bravery of his hero. And love, the indispensable ingredient of these novels, seems more poignant, more imperilled, more noble and self-sacrificing, when set against the backdrop of war.

The Sanctuary, by George Ward Nichols, published in 1866, epitomizes the qualities that most appealed to the Victorian lady reader. Nichols had served as aide-de-camp on the staff of General William Sherman from the fall of Atlanta in 1864 to the end of the war. From his diary he compiled *The Story of the Great March*, an account of the march to the sea, the subsequent campaign in the Carolinas, and the surrender of General Albert Johnston. His book, an instant success from the time of its publication in 1865, sold sixty thousand copies within a year. But instead of leaving well enough alone, Nichols decided to try his hand at fiction.

From the opening scene, showing federal troops in pursuit of General John Hood through northern Alabama, to the novel's close, when the bells of victory blend

By IRENE M. PATTEN

with wedding bells, Nichols crams *The Sanctuary* with incident. The characters suffer a breathless number of vicissitudes for the sake of love and patriotism before they are all—well, almost all—safely sheltered beneath the sanctuary, the flag of the restored Union.

With singular ineptitude the author narrates the trials and tribulations of three pairs of lovers. The machinery of the novel creaks and threatens to break down, now going into reverse with an awkward flashback, now making a jolting leap between two scenes widely separated in time or locale. Sometimes the reader is warned of an impending transition by some such phrase as "We left Major Dalton, at the close of our first chapter . . .," but more often the scene simply shifts.

David Dalton and Agnes Saumur are the Leading Lovers. Major Dalton is a Georgian whose family has remained loyal to the Union. As well as commanding troops in the northern cause, he has two other pressing problems. The first one concerns Agnes, a Savannah belle who refuses to marry him and forsake the Confederacy. At the time of their parting in 1861, Agnes makes her position clear:

"I will bear all the suffering. Whatever destiny is reserved for the South, I will share," and she looked heroically proud, her heart within her all the while melting with love for David Dalton. "You may be right," she continued, "but to me it seems criminally wrong. I cannot follow you. I cannot be the wife of a recreant to our cause."

Dalton's other problem is the search for his Lost Brother. Harold Dalton, forcibly conscripted into the Confederate Army, deserts, is recaptured, and is imprisoned in Savannah. There Agnes discovers him and is permitted to nurse the wounds he received at the time of his capture. For a time it appears that both problems may be solved at once when David, attempting to arrange Harold's release by means of an exchange of prisoners, encounters the noble Agnes. Although her heart has softened toward him, war has toughened his fiber. Agnes, about to tell him of her change of heart, realizes that he has not forgiven her:

But—and she, poor child, *must* see it now—there was scarcely recognition in the stern gaze which met her own, and what there was was like the light which momentarily flashes across the rain-clouds, and leaves them again as dark and forbidding as before.

The situation looks hopeless indeed when Agnes, no longer able to nurse Harold (who has been taken away by the retreating Confederate forces), flees to the North, certain that her love will never relent:

Her eyes are fixed upon the spires of the church under whose shadow she had glided—oh, so joyously!—from childhood into womanhood. . . . a film covers the lady's eye, coming between her and this fading vision. The ship has gone out upon the broad ocean, and Agnes Saumur has bidden adieu to home, to love, and to David Dalton.

Eventually, of course, everything falls into place. In rapid succession the brothers are reunited, the South surrenders, and so does Agnes. Nichols really lets himself go in the lushly romantic scene of the lovers' reunion. Let us not go into the twists and turns of plot that finally bring the lovers together, but the meeting finally does occur—at a performance of an opera in New York City. As they sit absorbed in Meyerbeer's *Les Huguenots*, Agnes sees her beloved, who remains unaware of her presence:

And when the curtain rose upon the final scene, and the two lovers, kneeling in the presence of Death, with exquisite melody sang the last sad song of love, Dalton, with his own sad longings, could bear no more, and turned his moistened eyes from the scene. And Agnes, at the same instant, animated by the same emotion, unmindful of the place, conscious only that Dalton was there, and that he sincerely loved her, half rose from her seat, turned, and the lovers were face to face.

"Agnes!"

"David!"

Electrified, each gazed in the other's eyes. In the moment of silence which followed, there was sanctified between David Dalton and Agnes Saumur that perfect marriage of the soul, all-comprehending, eternal.

But Nichols is not content with a two-handkerchief ending. He goes for three handkerchiefs and a resounding anticlimax by having Agnes murmur a place of rendezvous for the morrow before she flees into the night. The final, the grand, reconciliation takes place at an estate on the banks of the Hudson where Agnes is staying with relatives, and—believe it or not—as David clasps her in his arms, the sun sinks slowly in the west!

David's comrade-in-arms, Major Alfred Horton, and the blue-blooded Bostonian, Kate Noble, are the Supporting Lovers. While Alfred serves with Sherman in Georgia, Kate loyally resists the blandishments of Harry Gray, who stays at home to do a spot of war profiteering. At length the villain is foiled and true love rewarded when Alfred returns, a conquering hero, and kisses away "the tears of joy which filled Kate's eyes."

But love does not always conquer, as the Tragic Lovers, Zimri and Charlotte, discover. Zimri, a handsome and intelligent slave, is the natural son of his owner and a quadroon slave woman. Zimri has good reason to hate his white half brother, General Ralph Buford, who lusts after Charlotte, Zimri's beautiful quadroon wife. Zimri courageously assists Sherman's soldiers whenever he can, his hatred of Ralph becoming a passionate desire for revenge when his half brother abducts Charlotte. In a spectacularly melodramatic episode that, nevertheless, contains more genuine emotion than any other scene in the book, Zimri sets fire to the cabin where Ralph has spent the night with Charlotte. Though the girl dies, her seducer escapes. In due course Zimri has his chance for revenge, but even as the slave chokes the life out of his half brother, the author cannot resist a small oration:

This was more than the struggle for life as between man and man—more than that between the seducer and the betrayed husband. The spirit of Freedom had the spirit of Slavery by the throat, and meant to strangle it to death. It was that kind of equality which does not require special legislation, but has its abiding power in the fact that it asserts itself. It was that terrible power which, with the consciousness of newborn freedom, springs into life full armed, and woe be to him who menaces that liberty, and seeks to re-enslave.

If Nichols seems to sound here like an advocate of black power, he more frequently patronizes or even caricatures the Negro. In general he depicts the slaves as simple-minded, deeply religious creatures, bowing to their godlike white saviors and even, according to the stereotype, possessing to a man a strong sense of rhythm. At one point he describes a group of Negroes as "sable disciples of Terpsichore." Only Zimri, who has far more white than Negro blood, seems to have real initiative and intelligence.

In *The Sanctuary* Nichols' women—cherished, angelic, chaste, unfalteringly noble, and not very smart—fit just as neatly into the accepted stereotypes of the late nineteenth century. For instance, in describing Agnes Saumur he refers to the tender sensibilities of Woman and speaks tactfully of her judgment as being "different" from that of Man.

As for the war, the background against which all of this melodrama is enacted, Nichols seems reluctant to remind his feminine readers too forcefully of the truth of General Sherman's famous pronouncement. "War is hell," but for the most part the author avoids depicting its true hellishness. The book contains many scenes of troops on the move, fording rivers and engaging the enemy, but of the real effects of Sherman's march the reader is given only rare and fleeting glimpses:

But here, where the man in arms treads, the fruit is blasted, the stalk withered. Your heart aches at the wanton waste. You ride swiftly by through deserted villages. You are deaf—for you must be—to the cries of fainting mothers covering their starved dead children among the ashes of homes once so happy.

General Sherman himself appears in the book as a Presence rather than as a fully developed character. As one might expect of a loyal aide-de-camp, Nichols portrays Sherman in flattering, almost reverential, terms. One close-up scene in the General's tent shows him as "a strange, grand figure" but emphasizes his Spartan habits and impatience with pretentious ceremony:

Her voice fluttered, and the words came brokenly from her white lips.

"... I ought not, David, and I can not be your wife."

Then she ... stood alone, beautiful in her self-immolation and with her divine resignation.

"Agnes," said Dalton, "could you look into my heart, you would see how supremely I honor you. God grant that I may live to prove to you that I love you. Let us have faith that we have both been saved for some better fate."

There was a pleading earnestness in his eyes which caused Agnes to tremble with uncontrollable emotion, and she covered her face with her hands....

—*Text and frontispiece from* The Sanctuary

This was no Roman consul nor modern emperor traveling in grand state, with pompous mien and brilliant retinue, but a citizen-general of the Republic . . . in the simplicity of an unselfish devotion to his country doing the work which lay before him.

The reader of Nichols' *Story of the Great March* discovers that he was capable of achieving plain style and straightforward narrative, a talent that the author carefully buries in writing his romance. Since *The Sanctuary* was so popular and is so typical of its genre, one can hardly accuse Nichols of misjudging the taste of his audience or blame him too harshly for so obviously catering to it.

If one were to pick *the* Civil War romance, the one novel written before 1900 that contained everything to delight the hearts of lady readers, he might well decide on John Esten Cooke's *Surry of Eagle's-Nest* (1866). Cooke was himself a glamorous figure, a Virginian with a distinguished war record, having served as an officer on Stonewall Jackson's staff.

Borne on at a furious speed upon his powerful white horse, Ashby dragged his adversary clear out of the saddle, never relaxed his clutch, and in a moment was beyond pursuit, still dragging his prisoner by the side of his horse.

May Beverley . . . is sitting now upon a mossy rock, beneath a little pine; and, looking down, with cheeks suffused in blushes, plays with the tassel of her belt, or with an autumn flower, which she has plucked beside the rock. . . . O pine-tree, never whisper what you heard or saw! There are things which the cold world laughs at, makes its cynical jest of, and so desecrates.

Cooke, like Nichols, was well aware that the majority of his readers would be ladies. On nearly every page he addresses his audience as "dear reader," "my fair reader," or "mesdames" and pays tribute to southern womanhood on a number of occasions:

> Do not the prayers of women shield us often? I think so. They prayed with all their hearts in the late revolution, and were angels to us all. The soldiers of the army and the women did their duty; had the rest done likewise, we might have been the founders of an empire!

The author has omitted nothing to make feminine readers sigh and swoon. There are heroes enough for several books: Philip Surry, whose military career resembles Cooke's own, is a descendant of cavaliers who leaves his ancestral home, Eagle's-Nest, to fight for Virginia; Mordaunt—darkly handsome, mysterious, Byronic—after wandering the world as a soldier of fortune, has returned to fight for the Confederacy. What female heart

These three overheated passages from Surry of Eagle's-Nest *were illustrated by Winslow Homer in 1866.*

would not throb to read "that some great tragedy had darkened this man's life—some mortal poison embittered a character grand, noble, and magnanimous"?

Most heroic of all are the Great Captains of the Confederacy: Jeb Stuart, cavalier par excellence, now singing to the music of a banjo, now receiving garlands from southern maidens, but above all, Stuart, "the splendid war-machine"; Turner Ashby on his milk-white horse, fighting his way from Strasburg up the Shenandoah Valley, the general of whom Surry says, "I loved and admired him as the pearl of honor, the flower of chivalry." Surry's particular hero is General Jackson, no longer "Fool Tom," but Stonewall—eccentric, deeply religious, indomitable. Surry is with him when he receives his death wound while reconnoitering at night near Chancellorsville, accidentally shot by some of his own troops. After Jackson's death Surry calls him "the idol of the Southern people," "this man of destiny," and bemoans his loss:

> The form of Jackson had vanished from the scene: that king of battle had dropped his sword, and descended into the tomb: from that moment the star of hope, like the light of victory, seemed to sink beneath ebon clouds.

Such a plethora of heroes would seem to require at least two or three villains, but there is only one, Fenwick. More malignant than Shakespeare's Richard III, he is an all-round, multipurpose villain—seducer, blackmailer, forger. And that is not all. The war having ended when Cooke wrote his book, the author probably hoped to appeal to many northern readers, and he assigned to Fenwick evil tasks that, in other pro-Confederate books, were performed by Yankees. This protean scoundrel is thus a renegade southerner turned Union spy. With the possible exception of Sherlock Holmes's enemy, Professor Moriarty, Fenwick may be the most durable villain in literature. As early as Chapter VI he is shot in a duel by his sworn enemy, Mordaunt:

> If the bullet of his adversary had passed the one-thousandth part of an inch nearer to the femoral artery, the wound would have instantly proved fatal.

But he recovers, later to cross swords by the light of the moon with Mordaunt, who backs him up against a gigantic oak:

> Rushing upon him, with his sabre at tierce point, Mordaunt drove the keen weapon through his breast, and the point was buried in the tree beyond.

Again Fenwick survives to go about his dirty work, grinding his teeth and shaking his fists the while.

The nineteenth-century ladies who filled their parlors with massive, ornate furniture and fancy bric-a-brac wanted their novels to be equally crammed with plot, and Cooke was not the man to disappoint them. As the story opens, Philip Surry receives his commission as a captain, falls in love with May Beverley, and observes the first duel between Mordaunt and Fenwick. May, pledged to marry the wastrel Baskerville though she does not love him, is the kind of heroine every lady reader would have liked to be, unassailably virtuous and peerlessly beautiful. Surry first sees her in Richmond:

> Fancy a maiden of about nineteen, with a figure rounded,

CONTINUED ON PAGE 109

Mordaunt drove him, step by step, across the road, toward a gigantic oak, which stretched its gnarled branches above, in the moonlight—and then, with his back against the trunk, Fenwick could retreat no further.

The moon shone full upon his face—it was distorted by an expression which might have done honor to the mythologic furies. He struck at Mordaunt with the fury of despair—then the combat terminated.

Rushing upon him, with his sabre at tierce point, Mordaunt drove the keen weapon through his breast, and the point was buried in the tree beyond.

THE CIVIL WAR
AS MEMORIES

Year by year the ranks of the G.A.R. *grew thinner —but until the last old soldier was gone, Decoration Day in a New England town was a moving memorial to "the War"*

Harper's Young People, MAY 24, 1887

The Old Vets

By ROBERT MERRILL DEWEY

The War had been over hardly two decades when I was a boy. If one had occasion to refer to it, he called it simply "the War," for it was the only war we had had within the memory of all but a negligible few. School books like John Fiske's *History of the United States* called it "the Civil War." Histories for adults called it "the Great Rebellion." To call it "the Rebellion" in a school book would have confused the pupils, who would have found it hard to distinguish between "Rebellion" and "Revolution." In fact, years later I came upon a student at my university who thought them one and the same war. "The War Between the States" hadn't been coined, and it still sounds odd to nineteenth-century ears.

Our New England town had erected a Memorial Hall of brick with stone trim to honor its sons who had taken part in the conflict. On bronze mural tablets in the foyer are the names of those who lost their lives and of the battles in which they fell. On pedestals, one on each side of the wide flight of granite steps leading to the main entrance, stand heroic bronze statues by a now-forgotten sculptor—the one on the left, a soldier with his musket, standing at parade rest; the one on the right, a sailor, his right hand on the hilt of his cutlass, his left resting lightly on his hip. But what I liked best as a young child was the fieldpiece, a ponderous memento of the great struggle that stood on the lawn before the hall, aimed point-blank at the stores on the opposite side of Main Street. It was my delight to clamber over this monstrous relic or to sit astride its barrel, now forever silent.

In 1868 General John A. Logan, Commander in Chief of the Grand Army of the Republic, issued a general order designating May 30 of that year "for the purpose of strewing with flowers or otherwise decorating the graves of comrades who died in defense of their country during the late rebellion and with the hope that it will be kept up from year to year." This proposal met with approval by a public that still felt the loss of loved ones. Thereafter, May 30 was known as Decoration Day, until in 1882 the Grand Army urged that the proper designation of May 30 is Memorial Day. By that time, however, the term "Decoration Day" was fixed in the popular vocabulary, so that even now, those of my generation still use it.

In any case, by whatever name the day might be called, it belonged to the Veterans. All business was suspended. Stores, offices, and factories were closed. School did not keep. In fact, everything was at a standstill. Flags flew from all public buildings and from very many private dwellings.

On the last day of school before Decoration Day, in all classrooms there were "exercises." Boys and girls from the smarter half of the class recited "The Blue and the Gray," "O Captain! My Captain!" "Sheridan's Ride," and "Barbara Frietchie." In the ninth grade the smartest boy recited the Gettysburg Address. The parents of those pupils who took part attended the exercises, sitting at the front of the room, to the discomfort of their offspring. The class as a whole sang "The Battle Hymn of the Republic," "Tenting Tonight," "Columbia, the Gem of the Ocean," and "America" —"God Bless America" and "America the Beautiful" were yet to be composed. There was always a Veteran sent by the local Grand Army post to speak to us about loyalty, patriotism, and other abstractions. One of these had actually seen, with his very own eyes, the Great Emancipator himself. When the Veteran had spoken, the prettiest girl in the class, dropping a curtsy, presented him with a nosegay, which he awkwardly accepted. Then the class sang "The Star-Spangled Banner," and school let out for the day.

I used to wish that these speakers from the G.A.R. post would tell us about the War and what it was like to go into battle, but this never happened until some years later, when I was a student in high school and all four classes assembled in the auditorium for the exercises. By then the Veterans were getting old.

On that occasion, when the G.A.R. speaker rose from his seat on the platform and advanced stiffly to the lectern, his face was flushed and his eyes wore an inward look as though his thoughts were far away. To my delight he launched into a series of personal recollections—of marches and bivouacs, of advances and retreats under fire, of bayonet charges and hand-to-hand fighting. His memory was still clear; in fact, he seemed to have the faculty of total recall, and as he warmed to his subject, his imagination took fire. For upward of half an hour he ran on, while the principal, a gentleman and a scholar of the old school, grew more and more uneasy. Pointing his finger at the freshmen, who sat in the front rows, the speaker declared that were he to lead a company into battle, he would choose to lead just such youngsters as these. At length he stopped abruptly, turned about, and made his way a trifle unsteadily back to his seat. Of the many Decoration Day speeches that I listened to in my school days, this is the one I remember.

In the afternoon and evening before Decoration Day the wives and daughters of the Veterans, who constituted the ladies' auxiliary of the post, assembled in the G.A.R. headquarters to make bouquets with which to decorate the graves of the fallen in the ancient town cemetery. People who raised flowers contributed them in great quantities. No doubt the local florists also donated generously as a matter of patriotism and good will. We children brought bunches of wildflowers, hoping to be rewarded with one of the homemade doughnuts that, with coffee, were provided for the workers. The members of the auxiliary corps made the flowers into bouquets and stacked them in wooden washtubs half filled with water, to keep them fresh until the morrow.

On the morning of Decoration Day, which seldom failed to be sunny, the members of the Grand Army post assembled on the steps of Memorial Hall for their photograph. I have before me, as I write, a reproduction of one of these taken about the turn of the century, with about four-score Veterans in the picture. Perhaps the most remarkable thing about it is the disparity in their ages. Some look surprisingly young for men of at least middle age. These must have gone into the War when it was about over, or at an early age—drummer boys were accepted in their mid teens.

These youthful drummer boys were ready-made heroes for the tide of juvenile War fiction that followed the cessation of hostilities. By the time I had learned to read, they were well on their way out of fashion; but such books, tattered and dog-eared, were still to be borrowed at the public library. I believe I read every one there available and derived from them such inspiration that, when our war with Spain came along, I was greatly disappointed that drummer boys were no longer a part of the military.

Of the older Veterans, some look frail and shrunken; others, among whom are many with patriarchal beards or other whiskers, look hail and hearty despite their advanced years. Those intending to march in the parade to the cemetery wear military caps with visors or their soft black felt hats with the Grand Army insignia. The officers are wearing belts and swords. All wear their medals.

After the taking of the photograph the Veterans fell in behind the local fife and drum corps and marched with muffled drums to the cemetery. Those who had become too feeble to march or who suffered from old wounds rode in horse-drawn hacks with tops down, behind the ranks of their sturdier comrades. At the cemetery the Veterans and the women and children placed flowers and new flags on the graves of the former comrades-in-arms. A cast-iron G.A.R. emblem marked each grave permanently. At the plot reserved by the town, on which a monument had been erected "to the memory of soldiers sleeping in unknown graves," there was a brief service, with the customary three volleys by a firing squad and taps. Then the Veterans marched back to headquarters to the lively tune of "The Girl I Left Behind Me" or "When Johnny Comes Marching Home."

There was a supper that evening in Grand Army Hall, prepared and served by the ladies' auxiliary, at which the comrades who hadn't seen one another for the past twelvemonth got together and recalled almost-forgotten events. It had been their day.

By the time I was old enough to remember, the Veterans had long since become re-established in their respective vocations and were not distinguishable from the rest of the citizenry except on those occasions when they wore their old uniforms. Some, like Henry Childs, who for many years had operated a bookbindery, had retired. Mr. Childs was a regular customer at my father's tavern; so regular, in fact, that my father had placed a small wooden box in a nook inside the front entrance, where, after his mile walk downtown, the old man might sit and rest and watch the passers-by on Main Street. He was there almost every day for his one toddy; and when I came along with my little toy gun, he seldom failed to put me through the manual of arms.

Many Veterans had become storekeepers, like Alvin Rust, who had had erected on Main Street a three-story brick building, in the ground floor of which he kept a grocery store. But of all these Main Street establishments run by Veterans, the most interesting was the Clark & Parsons drugstore.

George Dexter Clark, whom I knew well in his old age, was a Veteran, as was, I believe, his partner, Mr. Parsons. The latter was in appearance a Victorian gentleman of business, carefully dressed in cutaway and high stiff collar, and dignified in manner. Mr. Clark dressed more casually, wore a stubbly, short red beard, and was of a friendly disposition. Their pharmacy was next door to the Mansion House, the town's leading hotel. The store had an entrance between two show windows, in each of which was a huge glass globe of colored water, one red, the other blue—the signs of a drugstore in the nineteenth century.

Within on the left was a handsome pink marble soda fountain, with half a dozen high stools before it. Except for this concession to the times the store was devoted to the proper business of pharmacy. It was entirely free of the innumerable articles that clutter the modern drugstore. There was not even a rack for magazines or picture post cards.

Beyond the cases, running across the store from wall to wall, was a wooden screen with opaque glass panels, behind which was the prescription counter. Beyond that was a rear room, in the center of which stood a potbelly stove surrounded with wooden armchairs and an occasional cuspidor. This back room became in time the unofficial gathering place of the Republican establishment of the community. Mr. Clark himself was a perennial member of the School Committee, a minor elective political office.

When he was a very old man, Mr. Clark told me that in the War he had contracted dysentery, from which he had suffered ever since. Many of the Veterans bore battle scars; some still carried in their bodies bullets that had not been removed. It was traditional, when the weather was about to get cold or stormy, that these wounds would ache.

Politics and the various forms of civil service attracted many of the returning soldiers. A Veteran had an advantage over a rival candidate who had not taken part in the War. When our town became a city in 1884, its first mayor was a Veteran, Benjamin Cook. On his return from the War he had gone into business as a junior partner with his father, a silversmith, jeweler, and mender of clocks and watches.

Egbert I. Clapp, one of those crippled in the War, was elected to the office of city clerk, to which he was re-elected unopposed year after year until he chose to retire. He walked with the assistance of a pair of handsome mahogany crutches that accorded with the fastidiousness of his dress. In their use he had become so adept that he skimmed over the ground faster than most men could walk.

Then there were those who had chosen to enter one or another form of civil service. Alfonso Witherell had shouldered one of the leather mailbags of the U.S. Post Office and twice a day trod his appointed round—altogether some ten miles. Luke Day had been made keeper of the lockup, outside of which in mild weather he usually sat at ease in his captain's chair. John Mercier had become head farmer at the state hospital for the insane. Mr. Farr (I never knew his first name) had been made head janitor of the public schools.

At least three Veterans had returned from the War with the rank of captain (or "cap'n," as we pronounced it): Cap'n Ed Clark, a slender, genteel man with white hair and beard who became president of the local street railway company; Cap'n Ed Hall, a large man with a luxuriant flowing blond mustache, the owner of a lumberyard in the very heart of the city; and Cap'n Hubbard Abbott, the registrar of probate. Their military titles clung helpfully to them throughout the rest of their lives.

Henry S. Gere had become the publisher of the *Gazette*, the local newspaper. Our neighbor Martin Van Buren Flagg had become a peripatetic optician, earning his living and that of his considerable family by peddling spectacles out of a satchel hung by a strap from his shoulder.

CONTINUED ON PAGE 108

The GI cartoonist Bill Mauldin as he looked in 1944, when he was photographed on the job in Rome.

For a gag, Bill Estoff, left, listed himself as a bookie. He became the paper's circulation manager.

The Stars and Stripes *staff takes off to collect news of the war. Author Herbert Mitgang is the driver.*

The model war journalist Ernie Pyle (with another correspondent at his left) chats with General Patton.

Newspaper work back home was never like this: the Stars and Stripes *staff does setting-up exercises.*

AT WAR WITH THE STARS AND STRIPES

Army newspapers in World War II were unofficial, informal, and more than the top brass could handle

By HERBERT MITGANG

In the summer of the year 1944, in a time of world war that is already history to my children's generation but remains vividly personal to mine as a moment of (in retrospect) astonishing simplicity and idealism, I found myself pointing a jeep in the direction of Pisa and Florence. On the so-called forgotten front in Italy, the *Wehrmacht* held the northern side of these cities; the line dividing their riflemen and ours was the river Arno.

The big show of the European war was being played out on the newly opened second front in Normandy. Along the French Riviera a diversionary side show became popularly known as the champagne war. Since the German 88's had not been informed that our Mediterranean theater had lessened in strategic importance, they were still to be reckoned with.

My windshield was down and covered with tarpaulin—any fool knew that glass reflected and could draw artillery fire or even a *Luftwaffe* fighter seeking a target of opportunity. I was driving along happily and singing to myself because all I needed was in that jeep: a Springfield rifle, a scrounged .25-caliber Italian automatic, two large cans of gasoline, one helmet (I wore the liner as a sunshade and the heavy steel pot, useful for shaving and washing, rattled around in the back), several days' worth of C and K rations, five gallons of water and two canteens of vino, and—most important of all—one portable typewriter.

That little Remington was the telltale of my military trade: I was an Army correspondent for *Stars and Stripes*, Mediterranean. Below the masthead of two enfolded flags its only mission was inscribed: "Daily Newspaper of the U.S. Armed Forces published Monday through Saturday for troops in Italy." Although we were occasionally enjoined to do so, we were not supposed to propagandize, publicize generals, or even inform and educate. Our job was to put out a newspaper as professionally as we could. Although armed, the soldier-correspondent was not necessarily expected to go looking for the enemy but instead to report about the soldiers, sailors, and airmen who did.

As I drove along the seacoast road, noticing the island of Elba at one point but without worrying about Napoleon or anyone else's war, the parting words of one of the correspondents came to mind. "Don't forget," he said, "your job is to get back stories, not get yourself killed." Two of my colleagues, Sergeants Gregor Duncan and Al Kohn, had died covering the front, and all of us were shaken up when what was an everyday occurrence in combat outfits struck home.

There were stories everywhere. My immediate problem was not to be distracted before reaching the Fifth Army's pyramidal tents. Ernie Pyle, whose influence as the most important single reporter at home and abroad of the Second World War cannot be exaggerated, had dignified the GI and the "little picture" in his syndicated newspaper column. I recalled having a drink with Pyle near the end of the Tunisian campaign in North Africa and could see part of his strength as an ingratiating reporter. He was skinny, wet, and shivering—a civilian version of the rifleman without rank, and therefore to be trusted.

None of us on *Stars and Stripes* deviated very much, or cared to, from his kind of reporting. Most of our seasoned front-line reporters, such as Jack Foisie, Ralph Martin, Stan Swinton, and Paul Green, roamed the field as Pyle did, covering not only battles but the "mess-kit repair battalions" (as the stray outfits were jokingly called) that supported the infantry. When I saw a sign that intrigued me—an outfit running a GI laundry somewhere near Leghorn—I stopped briefly, made a few notes for "flashes," chiselled some gasoline for my half-empty tank, and remembered to keep going.

After getting a tent assignment and a briefing at Fifth Army headquarters, which was located in a forest near a village somewhere between Pisa and Florence (whose name I cannot recall, though I vividly remember a long evening's talk with the parish priest about the art of the carillonneur and how his bell ringing regulated life and death), I decided to look in on something called an "armored group." It consisted of a self-sufficient group of tanks, artillery, engineers, and riflemen—a forerunner of the integrated, brigade-size units several chiefs of staff assumed would work for the brush-fire wars of the future.

The artillerymen appeared to be most active that afternoon. They were maintaining their franchise by firing harassing shells across the Arno. I took my names and hometown addresses, listened to the battery commander explain his "mission" in stiff Army lingo, and then accepted the captain's invitation to try out the armored group's mess for dinner. What happened next sticks with me as an example of the confusion that existed right in our own theater about *Stars and Stripes* correspondents. I immediately noticed that the two long tables were divided between field-grade officers (colonels, lieutenant colonels, and majors) and company-grade officers (captains and lieutenants). The colonel directed me to sit with him and motioned the captain to sit with his ignoble kind.

There was only one slight error in seating rank here: I, like most correspondents on *Stars and Stripes*, was a lowly sergeant. By the rules of the Army game I was not supposed to be waited upon at either of these tables, but instead to be somewhere out in the field with a mess kit in which the Spam floated around in the brown gravy and peach juice. One lieutenant colonel—to be on the safe side—kept sirring me. I waited for the inevitable to happen, trying to postpone it at least until the dessert. Finally, after a series of questions, the colonel nearest me asked pointblank: "Are you fellows on *Stars and Stripes* civilians or soldiers?" I mumbled something to the effect that we were soldiers but operated in the same manner as the civilian correspondents. He pursued: "Then what's your rank?" Swallowing, I said: "Staff sergeant." Nothing, of course, happened, the embarrassment being all on my side.

The reason for the confusion was that we carried a patch on our left sleeve saying "Stars and Stripes," without any mark of rank. This was by design. I recall a meeting of the *Stars and Stripes* staff in the Red Cross building on the Boulevard Baudin, Algiers, where we lived and worked. Several of the correspondents had just returned from the Tunisian front. An opportunity existed for some members of *Stars and Stripes* to be commissioned. One already had been—James Burchard, a former sportswriter for the New York *World-Telegram*, who was in his late thirties (most of us were in our twenties).

Lieutenant Burchard and two sergeants described their reporting experiences. The lieutenant said that in order to get GI's to speak to him freely he had to take his bars off and put them in his pocket; he did find the bars useful for eating and pulling rank for transportation.

As a result we decided to avoid commissions because correspondents could perform better as enlisted men. Most of us did not wear our sergeant's stripes precisely because we wanted to foster the impression that we were—or at least until discovered—as privileged and possibly as talented as the regular civilian correspondents (whose pay greatly exceeded ours). I always liked to think of it this way: a *Stars and Stripes* reporter could honestly interview himself and, without fear of contradiction, say he had talked to a GI.

Although *Stars and Stripes* did have commissioned officers on the staff, they were mainly engaged in administrative duties. A specific difficulty arose when I was managing editor of the combined Oran-Casablanca edition of *Stars and Stripes*. A cast-off first lieutenant was assigned to us to censor the mail, requisition food, sign pay vouchers, and so on. He had been pressured by a base-section colonel to run that bane of all military newspapers, "The Chaplain's Corner." I refused his demand to run it. Several days later our own *Stars and Stripes* commanding officer in North Africa, Colonel Egbert White, came down to Oran from Algiers and, rather bluntly in my presence, told the lieutenant that the sergeant who was managing editor had final say over the contents of the paper.

In nearly every other case involving this delicate issue of officer-and-enlisted-men relationships on *Stars and Stripes*, there was no awkwardness. Nearly everyone was on a first-name basis, regardless of rank. All of us were so pleased to be out of regular outfits that we gladly abandoned the normal military way.

Whenever another Mediterranean invasion was in the wind, everyone on the staff hoped to get a piece of the action. *Stars and Stripes* reporters were poised with different units before the invasion of Sicily, for example. Sergeant Ralph Martin went in with the Rangers; Sergeant Phil Stern, an ex-Ranger himself, took three hundred pictures with the Seventh Army; Sergeant Paul Green swept over the island in a B-25; Sergeant Jack Foisie started out with the airborne infantry and, in the middle of the Sicilian campaign, was the only correspondent to accompany a small American force that made an amphibious attack seven miles behind the enemy lines along the coast of northern Sicily.

By the time the Mediterranean edition of *Stars and Stripes* had followed the troops across to Sicily and then to Naples and Rome, it had gained the loyalty and affection of officers and enlisted men—Air Force and Navy as well as Army. I saw its importance even to generals when American troops crossed the Arno and entered Pisa.

Naturally everyone wanted a close look at the leaning tower. I went there for a special reason; I was sure that the figures I had seen walking around its upper floors from across the Arno were German observers. I looked for a trace of their presence and found it in a piece of their orange-colored signal wire still hanging down. This, despite their claims that they were not using the campanile because it was church property. I was negotiating with an Italian official to enter the locked tower when, in a flurry of jeeps, General Mark W. Clark, the Fifth Army commander, drove up.

An affable general who was never shy about his personal publicity, Clark looked around for correspondents to cover him as he assumed the role of conqueror of Pisa. None had yet reached Pisa—except the correspondent from *Stars and Stripes*. The General cordially shook my hand and said, "Sergeant, why don't we go up and take a look?" The General and I became the first Americans to do so. At the top he posed his hawklike profile for a Signal Corps photographer—but a wise colonel on his staff killed the picture on grounds that it might be used by the Germans as propaganda to show that *Americans* had turned the tower into an observation post.

COURTESY OF HERBERT MITGANG

Censorship and generals occasionally plagued *Stars and Stripes*. For the most part censorship was confined to military matters, such as making sure that fresh units were not identified until the enemy knew of their presence and strength. With this we, of course, did not disagree, since we were no more desirous of giving information to the Germans than was the censor. But when a story was held up for nonmilitary reasons, we complained.

I was impressed by the bravery, which almost reached the point of foolhardiness, of certain Italian partisans who were helping the Americans and British north of the Arno. When I wrote about them and their political radicalism, the story was stopped. I would resubmit it week after week, but that story never passed. On other occasions my colleagues and I learned how to circumvent censorship by planting in our copy certain obvious red flags that would be cut out in order to let other material stay in. These, in the main, centered on stories that revealed high-command clay feet.

While I was managing editor of the Sicilian edition of *Stars and Stripes*, probably the most sensitive story of the war fell into my lap. It was the incident in which General George S. Patton had slapped a hospitalized soldier. We knew about it, of course, but had a special problem (to put it mildly) in Sicily: General Patton and his Seventh Army headquarters were there. I had received a file of stories and matrixes from our weekly newspaper in North Africa and noticed that the Algiers edition had carried an AP story about the face-slapping incident. I thought this was the perfect solution. So I reprinted the wire-service story, put it under a fairly quiet two-column headline on the bottom of page 1, and submitted it to the major from Army headquarters assigned as censor. He gulped, read the story, and smiled weakly.

"This story presents a problem," he said. "Do you really want to run it?"

"Of course," I replied. "All I'm doing is picking up the wire-service report that already appeared in Algiers."

"But Patton is in Sicily," he said, "and he reads *Stars and Stripes* every morning with his breakfast. Can you imagine him reading this?"

I could, but argued, "The integrity of the paper is at stake. Because once this story appears in the States, families clip it out and mail it here. Then the GI's know we're suppressing news about their own theater."

The major seemed to see the light—for a moment. "I'd better check this with the colonel," he said. While I waited for my page proofs to be okayed, he called his next above. The major explained the story, then cupped the mouthpiece and whispered to me, "The colonel asked me to hang on while he checks with the General." I whispered, "Patton?" The major nodded and said, "Or Patton's chief of staff." Finally the voice came back on and the major signalled me to listen in with him.

"Major," I heard the colonel say coldly, "the answer is, It's *your* decision." The major hesitated, and then said, "Can you give me some guidance, sir?" The colonel replied, "Major, I would suggest that you use your own judgment based on what is best for the Army." He hung up. The major got the message. "My judgment is," he told me, "you can't run this story in Sicily." As I picked up my page proofs and left without a word, he said, "Dammit, I'm sorry."

Normally, being barless, stripeless, and in uniform had its advantages for the *Stars and Stripes* correspondent. The only instance in my own experience in which being an American soldier was the reason for not allowing me to cover a story occurred when the British reinvaded Greece in autumn of 1944. At the time I was covering Advanced Allied Force Headquarters (which wasn't very advanced —it was in Rome; the regular AFHQ was still back at the palace in Caserta). From a friend on the British *Eighth Army News*, our allied opposite newspaper, I learned that some civilian correspondents were going to be allowed to accompany the British, but no American soldiers would be included. The given reason was that Greece was to be strictly a British "show," on Prime Minister Churchill's orders. No American uniforms were desired on the scene to complicate the future political leverage that the Churchill government wanted to exercise there alone. Months later we discovered that this part of the world was being made safe for the "democracy" of the restored Greek royal house.

When I requested permission to accompany the British 2nd Parachute Brigade on the operation, I was politely refused. Then I heard that the U.S. 51st Wing would carry the chutists. I argued that they could not prevent me from covering just the American C-47's taking part in the jump. A compromise was worked out: I would be allowed to go along but not to land in Greece. We took off from a base in southern Italy, flew across the Ionian Sea and along the Gulf of Corinth, and arrived in sunlight at the drop zone—a small airfield at Megara, west of Athens. Apparently the retreating Germans knew we were coming and had mined the field, but the Greek partisans, who included many Communists, had saved many lives by unarming the mines. The quite wonderful British "red devils" (whose berets were maroon, actually) hit the silk (not nylon, then) and fell to earth without losing a man; I had the privilege of joining them—because who would know otherwise in Megara?

After interviewing people on the ground and getting such vitally unimportant information as the fact that most of the Greek partisans I spoke to seemed to have brothers who owned restaurants in the States, I wrote my stories. Later, at Advanced AFHQ, I had to honor my end of the bargain by such devious datelines as "With the 51st Wing over Greece"—which, curiously, included talks with Athenians on the ground. More important than the stories, however, I brought back one of the ripped silk chutes to Rome, and a seamstress there made dozens of scarves for my *Stars and Stripes* colleagues to wear around their olive-drab throats that winter of 1944–45 in Italy.

Nearly all staffers had come to *Stars and Stripes* from other outfits by hook, crook, or luck. The Mediterranean edition had begun to publish in Algiers on December 9, 1942, a month after the North African landings. It had been preceded by a London edition—the first of World War II—that started on April 18, 1942.

The British edition was Air Corps oriented, because that was the only war they had to write about for more than two years, until the second front was opened in Normandy. Our edition was, from the beginning, infantry oriented. Not being stationed in England, we were also more politically aware around the Mediterranean, because our basic story was the rise of France overseas and the fall of Italian fascism. By the time we reached Rome we were putting out a newspaper that was superior to many dailies in the United States to this day. It was eight pages long; later, twenty-four on Sunday, including a magazine, a news review, and color comics—a mechanical achievement we were proud of. All of us spent many a Saturday night folding in the comics by hand for the Sunday paper.

We were lucky to have two unusual men to guide the Mediterranean edition administratively and editorially—Egbert White, who had been a private first class on the First World War *Stars and Stripes* and, after an advertising and publishing career, had entered the Army a second time; and Robert Neville, a journalist who had specialized in foreign news as editor and correspondent for the New York *Herald Tribune*, *Time* magazine, and the adless newspaper, *PM*. In retrospect, what made them outstanding was that they not only knew their business but also had a high level of tolerance about the staff. Many of the young men they took on had little experience, but White and Neville were willing to take chances, defend whims, and deflect the Army brass.

Around the Mediterranean the editions included personnel from every department of a newspaper but the pressroom. We had our own photographers, engravers, linotypists, and make-ups. In the mechanical area the GI printers and specialists often worked side by side with French and Italian craftsmen, and there was great mutuality of interest. The administrative officers and editors worried about the paper from the time it was raw stock, shipped from the States, till it was printed and distributed. The paper's circulation was handled by Sergeant William Estoff, who used everything from mules to C-47's for deliveries. Outfits near the city where the paper was printed usually picked up their quotas with their own transportation. Our own *Stars and Stripes* trucks rode through the night to deliver the paper to front-line divisions north of Rome and Air Corps wings south of Naples. The paper cost two francs or two lire in rear areas but was distributed free at the front.

Some of the soldiers who applied for transfer to *Stars and Stripes* came right out of combat units during the Tunisian and Italian campaigns. In the case of the GI printers, Sergeant Irving Levinson, our mechanical superintendent, went looking for them, but it was usually the other way around for correspondents and editors. In either case the men knew what they were writing, editing, or printing, for they had been in line outfits themselves.

The way I joined *Stars and Stripes* was typically untypical. I had been in southern Algeria with an Air Corps wing. When time allowed I put out a mimeographed paper called *The Bomb-Fighter Bulletin*, its news literally pulled out of the air by monitoring the BBC and Radio Berlin. I accidentally saw a copy of *Stars and Stripes* and decided to apply for a job. With the help of a kind lieutenant from my unit who covered up for me, I went A.W.O.L. for two days and showed up in Algiers, where *Stars and Stripes* had its office. I was interviewed by Neville, then a harassed lieutenant, who moaned that he was having trouble finding solid newspapermen (which I certainly was not). Then he said, "Do you know that there are people on this paper who don't know how to spell Hitler's first name?" I trembled, fearing he might ask me, and I wouldn't know whether he wanted it to end in *f* or *ph*. Fortunately he didn't ask, and a month or so later I received my transfer.

The story of how William Estoff, our circulation chief, got on *Stars and Stripes* was cherished by his friends as the definitive exposé of shavetails and military foul-ups. One day in England a call came to a replacement depot for an enlisted man with newspaper circulation experience. A lieutenant dutifully examined the service records. He suddenly stopped at the name Estoff, private; age, mid-thirties; civilian occupation, bookmaker. (Estoff, a night-club and newsstand operator, as a lark had listed himself as a bookie.) "Bookmaker," the lieutenant is reported to have said. "That sounds close to what *Stars and Stripes* needs. Books—newspapers—can't be too different." Thus started a career for Sergeant Estoff that resulted in getting the ideal man for the complex assignment of making sure that the paper was circulated quickly to front-line divisions, plus the Air Corps and Navy.

As the war progressed, seasoned journalists—Hilary Lyons, Howard Taubman, John Radosta, John Willig, all past or future members of the *New York Times*—helped to turn the Mediterranean edition into a newspaper with a serious approach to U.S. and world events. Wire-service reports became available but were not accepted at face value. The major stories—our Italian front, northern Europe, the Russian counteroffensive, the Pacific theater—were handled on our own copy desk. The need was seen for better reporting from Washington and the home front slanted to an Army newspaper for men overseas, many of whom had missed three Christmases home. One correspondent began to be rotated every four or five months; from where we sat in Algiers or Palermo or Rome, we referred to our man in New York as the "foreign correspondent in reverse." Sergeant Bill Hogan was assigned to his home town, San Francisco, to report the founding of the United Nations there.

The *Stars and Stripes* in the Second World War leapfrogged the rear echelons. Thirty different editions were published; a number were dailies. Combined readership ran into the millions. As the Army freed each new island or town or country, editors, printers, and circulation men rushed into the nearest newspaper plant, occasionally at gunpoint, and took over. One of our lieutenants entered the plant of the *Giornale di Sicilia*, found the reluctant owner, and decided to put a fresh clip into his .45 at the moment of hesitancy. The owner relented, and *Stars and Stripes* began printing in Palermo. On the day Rome was freed, a dash was made for the plant of *Il Messaggero* by Sergeant Milton Lehman and several others, and a paper, headlined "WE'RE IN ROME," was actually handed to some troops as they entered the city.

The news itself was supplemented by the two most popular features in the paper: "Puptent Poets" and "Mail Call." Although some distinguished poets in uniform were published, most of the men who submitted poems made no claim to expertise. There was humor ("Dirty Gertie from Bizerte/Hid a mousetrap 'neath her skirtie") and sentimental awareness ("This is the bridge. Dante stood in this place/And caught a fire that flamed Firenze town"). Corporal John Welsh III found himself doing little else but handling poetry on the Mediterranean edition; in two years one thousand poems were published, and fifteen times that were acknowledged with regret. In many cases poems were published posthumously. For the GI, poetry was the Greek chorus of his conscience, emerging in language of humor, protest, and even beauty.

The "Mail Call" column, edited by Sergeant Robert Wronker, exceeded the poetry in numbers received and printed. Initially, when *Stars and Stripes* published a new edition, the managing editor might write a few provoking letters under an assumed name to get the letters coming. What better way than to have a fictional "1st Sergeant McGonigle" demand more calisthenics for draftees overseas to keep them in trim as in the good old days of the prewar Regulars? What a private couldn't tell his supply sergeant and what a platoon lieutenant couldn't call a base-section saluting demon wound up in *Stars and Stripes* as a letter, poem, or article—and sometimes commanders listened, learned, restrained.

Bill Mauldin's daily cartoon reflected the paper's editorial attitude, yet he seldom editorialized. "Up Front . . . By Mauldin" was just that—a greatly talented soldier's view of what was on the combat GI's mind but not articulated until Mauldin expressed it for him in a simple sentence. He was in a direct line from the First World War's Bruce Bairnsfather, the British creator of the "Old Bill" cartoons and the play *The Better 'Ole*. One of Mauldin's early cartoons, showing the bearded Joe and Willie in an Italian foxhole, was captioned: "Th' hell this ain't th' most important hole in th' world. I'm in it." The Mauldin cartoons were not jokes; nor were they bitter humor. Rather, they were sardonic comments lifted out of the mouths and minds of front-line soldiers.

The cartoons invariably heroized the real dogface, often with a swipe at the rear echelon. In a cartoon that caused many soldiers to categorize themselves, Joe points to a couple of soldiers sitting at an outdoor café in France and comments, "We calls 'em garritroopers. They're too far forward to wear ties an' too far back to git shot." Mauldin's cracks were against oppressive authority, officer or EM.

Most of the generals—with a notable exception—enjoyed the Mauldin cartoons, defended them, sometimes asked for an original. But the cartoonist really stuck his neck out when he drew a cartoon ridiculing the tight discipline in the Third Army area—General George Patton's—that included a list of fines signed "By Order Ol' Blood and Guts."

An obligatory scene was played out between the General and the sergeant at Third Army headquarters. Captain Harry Butcher, General Eisenhower's naval aide, who arranged the confrontation, warned Mauldin to please wear a tidy uniform, stand at attention, and salute smartly. The General objected to the unkempt appearance of Willie and Joe; the sergeant said that he thought his characters faithfully represented the front-line GI. The meeting was a stand-off. Later, General Patton told Captain Butcher, "Why, if that little s.o.b. ever comes in the Third Army area again, I'll throw him in jail." Mauldin returned to Italy. Recalling the meeting long afterward, he told me, "I was frightened but steadfast."

Occasionally, in Naples, Mauldin would try out one of his caption lines on me. Rarely did I succeed in getting him to change a word—for a very good reason: his ear had perfect GI pitch. Who could improve upon the cartoon showing two stuffy officers overlooking a sunset and its accompanying line: "Beautiful view. Is there one for the enlisted men?"

There was a special reason why formal editorials were not needed. A positive tone characterized the paper. *Stars and Stripes* was not an "Army" newspaper—it did not exist between the two World Wars—but, instead, a creation and expression of civilians under arms. A most important influence—more so than any general—was President Franklin D. Roosevelt, who voiced the American dream in language understood by the ranks. The President's popularity was shown by the soldiers' ballots in the 1944 election.

The Four Freedoms speech delivered by Roosevelt, the inspiring speeches of Winston Churchill, the organization of the United Nations, were all fully reported in *Stars and Stripes*. The civilians in uniform who put it out

CONTINUED ON PAGE 108

Stars and Stripes in the First World War was the famous one, and justly so. From February 8, 1918, to June 13, 1919, its staff in Paris put out seventy-one fiercely independent, sentimental weekly issues. It was run by enlisted men—Private Harold W. Ross, Railway Engineers; Private John T. Winterich, Aero Service; Private Hudson Hawley, Machine Gun Battalion; Sergeant Alexander Woollcott, Medical Department—who were the editorial Big Four. Two officers—Captain Franklin P. Adams and Lieutenant Grantland Rice—for a time served as columnists. Many future journalists of distinction rounded out this brilliant staff, and outside poetry contributors included Sergeant Joyce Kilmer.

The formal authorization came in a message from General John J. Pershing that appeared on the first page of Volume 1, Number 1: "In this initial number of The Stars and Stripes, published by the men of the Overseas Command, the Commander-in-Chief of the American Expeditionary Forces extends his greetings through the editing staff to the readers from the front line trenches to the base ports. . . . The paper, written by the men in the service, should speak the thoughts of the new American Army and the American people from whom the Army has been drawn. Good luck to it."

It was only in the years after World War II that historical research uncovered casual editions of *Stars and Stripes* that existed even before the famous World War I edition. The first issue of the *Stars and Stripes* as a military paper appeared in Bloomfield, Missouri, on Saturday, November 9, 1861. This edition was published by Union soldiers of the 18th and 29th Illinois Volunteer regiments. Unfortunately the paper only appeared once, probably due to the exigencies of the war in the Union's Department of the West.

Other issues of soldier papers called *Stars and Stripes* were put out by men in blue during the Civil War. Each one was independent, and no links existed between these short-lived issues and Washington. A group of federal privates held in Confederate prisons in Richmond, Tuscaloosa, New Orleans, and Salisbury, North Carolina, for ten months before being exchanged in 1862 produced a hand-written *Stars and Stripes*. One of the offices where the paper was written was "Cell No. 9, third floor." Other independent editions of *Stars and Stripes* appeared in Jacksonport, Arkansas (the editor was post surgeon of the 3rd Cavalry Regiment of Missouri Volunteers), and in Thibodaux, Louisiana, in the local office of the Thibodaux *Banner* (whose owner had departed hurriedly) by Connecticut's 12th Regiment. Both editions were printed on wallpaper due to the shortage of newsprint.

On the Confederate side of the lines, peripatetic-soldier papers were published, too. One was called the *Daily Rebel Banner*, but there was no *Stars and Stripes*. —*H.M.*

In 1938 Faulkner posed in the uniform of his own airline. He was the chief (and only) pilot of a trimotor Stinson and other smaller craft.

John Faulkner's Vanishing South

John Faulkner, like his more famous brother William, was a novelist, but he was also a painter. During the decade before his death in 1963 he painted a series of oils and water colors that he called "Scenes of the Vanishing South," portraying his home town of Oxford, and Lafayette County, Mississippi. Some were painted from his memory of his boyhood, and others from the daily life of Beat Two, the hilly northeast sector of the county that is the scene also of most of his fiction. (A Mississippi county is composed of autonomous "beats," each under its elective supervisor of roads.) Having come upon hard times as a commercial airline pilot in Memphis, John moved to Beat Two in 1938 as manager of a farm William bought. It was a short-lived venture, being devoted to producing mules at a time when mules were already obsolete; but John began to write then and produced in time eight books of fiction as well as a number of short stories and a posthumously published book of reminiscences about William.

John Faulkner is affectionately remembered as a talented teller of tales, the best of which were likely to be about the densely idiosyncratic natives of Beat Two, and his paintings, like his novels, are anecdotal. He never sold the originals, which are in his wife's possession, but took orders for copies at exhibitions held in various Mississippi towns and in Memphis. (He liked to explain to customers that he got better with each effort.) He used the paintings as points of departure for his tales of the people and the history of Lafayette County, and he wrote, as people who heard him insist, just as naturally as he talked—though there was evidently more art in both the talking and the writing than they realized. The interplay of talk, writing, and painting was emphasized by his custom of posting explanatory "legends" with the paintings at exhibitions. He typed the legends, single-spaced, and tacked them beside the paintings, which he framed in unpainted pine.

Born in 1901, he was christened John Wesley Thompson Falkner III but adopted the spelling of the patronymic made famous by his brother, whose first book was published, through typographical error, as "by William Faulkner." John was educated at the University of Mississippi as a civil engineer and was employed for a time by the state highway department before becoming, like brothers William and Dean, a pilot. During the two years he managed the farm in Beat Two, he was also a supervisor for the Work Projects Administration. In this job he had to cope with the hillmen on the WPA rolls who, though no longer independent small farmers and hunters, still claimed as a masculine prerogative the right not to work. Out of this experience came John Faulkner's first published novel, *Men Working* (1941), a memorable blend of realism and macabre humor in which he broached what was to prove his major theme as a writer: the confrontation between the unreconstructed hill types he knew in Beat Two and the welfare state. After serving as a Navy officer in World War II, he returned to Oxford to live in his wife's family house—a pleasantly porched and roomy white frame building dating from 1838 and designed in what he described as bastard colonial. There he wrote and painted for the rest of his life.

Although overshadowed by his Nobel-laureate brother, John

By REDDING S. SUGG, JR.

Little Chicago

The roadhouse run by Mae and George that I write about in my books. It actually stood in the northeast corner of the county until the neighbor women rose up in wrath at the goings-on there and burned it down one night. It is night. One green-shaded droplight hangs from the rafters overhead. . . . You can see half-filled bottles and fruit jars [of whiskey] sitting about on the counter and juke box. Their favorite songs are "Birmingham Jail" and "The Letter Edged in Black." They cry over them when sung. However, tonight the juke box is stilled; the "Man in the Blue Suede Shoes" is there with his guitar. Elvis [Presley] actually played in the honky-tonks about the eastern edge of the county in his earlier days.

The Bear

Isaac "had a little dog . . . a mongrel, of the sort called fyce . . . possessing that sort of courage which had long since stopped being bravery and had become foolhardiness. He brought it with him one June and, timing them as if they were meeting an appointment with another human being . . . they lay downwind of the trail and actually ambushed the bear. . . . It turned at bay against the trunk of a big cypress, on its hind feet; it seemed to the boy that it would never stop rising, taller and taller. . . . Then he realized that the fyce was actually not going to stop. He flung the gun down and ran. When he overtook and grasped the shrill, frantically pinwheeling little dog, it seemed to him that he was directly under the bear."

—William Faulkner, "The Bear"

Faulkner produced a respectable body of fiction. *Men Working* was followed by *Dollar Cotton* (1942), a naturalistic novel about a hillman who makes and loses millions as a planter in the Delta, and by *Chooky* (1950), a book of loosely related tales for and about boys. Unfortunately, after that John began to publish his books as paperback originals that were not reviewed, although it can be argued that they are his mature and most distinctive works. Beginning with *Cabin Road* in 1951, he published in this way a series of five humorous novels about Beat Two characters, the other four being *Uncle Good's Girls* (1952), *The Sin Shouter of Cabin Road* (1955), *Ain't Gonna Rain No More* (1959), and *Uncle Good's Week-End Party* (1960). According to his publisher, more than two million copies of these books were sold. In them the predominant tone is one of hearty relish for the eccentric characters, their language—Faulkner was an accomplished speaker and writer of dialect—and their outlandish doings.

In his novels as well as his paintings John Faulkner does not sentimentalize the hillman, but idealizes him as historically a small subsistence farmer immune to the evils of money, the most immediate of which are seen in the speculative cotton farming that ruined land and man alike, with the consequent "blue government checks" of the WPA and later federal doles. In his heyday the hillman did not work for a living, but simply lived, raising the food and fiber needed for his family, supplementing his table by hunting and fishing, and cherishing his independence in a healthy, half-ritualistic relationship with the land and with nature. According to Faulkner, the hillman was devoted to values that were specifically "not for sale"; but with the triumph of industrialism after the Civil War, the boom in cotton prices toward the end of the century, and the opening up of the hills by railroad and highway the values of the metropolitan civilization proved irresistible.

Believing, as he said in a letter to his publisher in 1951, that human nature is essentially the same everywhere, while character or identity is a function of place and local conditions, Faulkner prized the vanishing peculiarities of his own region. In his paintings and his novels he attempted to record accurately, and to honor, a mode of human identity that was disappearing into the homogeneity of American life in the mid-twentieth century.

A truly "primitive" painter, Faulkner exhibits the qualities of primitive painting the world over—the flattened perspectives; the enlarged figure, used as a means of emphasis, such as that of the "Man in the Blue Suede Shoes" in *Little Chicago;* the rather crude but evocative delineation of human figures and faces. But he was duly modest about his painting, more concerned with the subject matter than with painting as such, and the charm of the results is no doubt in large part a reflection of his fascination with the distinctive humanity of Lafayette County and especially Beat Two.

Mr. Sugg, who is a leading authority on the works of John Faulkner, lives in Memphis, Tennessee, the metropolis nearest to Faulkner's Mississippi hill country. It was with his cooperation, and with the kind permission of Mrs. John Faulkner, that the selection from Faulkner's paintings on this and the following pages was made. With the exception of those for The Bear *(opposite) and* The House of Doom *(pages 74–75), the captions were written by John Faulkner himself.*

John Faulkner
1957

Brush Arbor

Brush arbor time is summertime, between laying by and harvest. That is when Negroes hold their revival meetings and conferences. They cut poles and erect what looks like a tent frame and cover it over the top with handy brush against the sun and weather. A pulpit is brought in a wagon from some nearby church. Logs are pulled in and used for seats. A single coal-oil lantern is swung by bailing wire from the ridge pole of the structure. The light is required for their night meetings. In this scene the preacher is in his pulpit making a stiff-fingered gesture toward heaven. It is night. The lantern is lit. A moon hangs in the sky above the arbor. A baby has crawled from its mother's lax attention and is at the foot of the pulpit looking up at the preacher's exhortations. A dog sits a few feet behind the baby, also attentive. The log seats are lined with the congregation. Two small boys fight on the ground between two of the logs. A woman is leaning forward trying to stop them. Those nearby have turned to look at the fight. One woman's husband, to the left, has dropped off to sleep, his head hanging forward. She is jabbing him in the side with her finger, trying to wake him up. One young couple, to the right, can be seen slipping from their end seats on the log into the friendly shadows. The back row is mostly couples with their arms around each other. Just inside the aisle, between the log ends, is a dog who, in passing, saw the dog listening to the preacher and is stalking his unsuspecting back. The young blacks are standing just in the shadows to the rear, not quite in the church. They have not removed their hats. They stand with their hands in their pockets, waiting for whatever might turn up.

John Faulkner

Git a Hoss

A scene of spring flowers. A Model T is stuck in the mud. Showers can be seen in the distance. They have already passed this way. The man is looking up the road with an axe in his hand. He has on high shoes of that day and is muddy half way up his calf. Logs he has cut lie about the rear wheel of the car. The tires are Pennsylvania Vacuum-cups. One farmer who is in rubber boots and has been down to see if his field was dry enough to plow squats beside the road. His dog sits beside him. An old Negro stoops behind the car looking at the wheel in the mud. A mule looks over the fence. I don't know which one knows the most about what they are looking at. A small boy is up the road, pointing back at the car, hollering to a farmer in a high field to come pull the car out of the mud. Two nearby cabins have women and children on the porch and in the yard looking toward the car. A dog and a small boy are running down the road. Water stands in the road and road ditches. The man's wife in the car has on a linen duster of that day. She has on a linen cap tied in place with a bright green scarf. Everyone is waiting for the small boy to "git a hoss."

John Faulkner

Sorghum Mill at Night

The nearest thing to voodoo I have ever seen. One of the Negroes came by the house one fall night and told us they were cooking sorghum up on the north end of the place. We went up. As we came down a hill to the little clearing this is what we saw. The only light they have is a fire on a square of tin nailed to the top of a post in the ground, and the red glare from the furnace under the "kittle" when the door is opened to stoke in more wood. Sorghum cooking is an inherited ability. The cooker is trained through an apprenticeship that lasts from the time he is old enough to tote wood to the furnace through "off-bearing" the pummins (squeezed-out sorghum stalks), feeding the mill, and finally graduating to "cooker." Even after graduation the old cooker holds sway. He is the only one who rates a chair. You see Uncle Jim Buddy Smith in the chair. His wife stands beside him. Charlie, whom Uncle Jim taught to succeed him, is testing for "string and snap." It is the high moment in the cooking. A dipper of sorghum is held between the cooker and the fire on the piece of tin on the post. The dipper is tilted the least bit. As soon as sorghum spills out the dipper is tilted back the other way, cutting off the stream. When the juice has cooked the right amount the stream parts with a "snap," and two bright golden threads curl back from the break. Everyone is looking at Charlie to see if he nods his head. Charlie is looking at Uncle Jim to see if he nods his. When the sorghum is ready it is poured up in gallon cans. The cooker gets a toll, for the whole neighborhood swears by its cooker and hauls its sorghum to his kettle. Two dogs can be seen at the skimming barrel where the foam is skimmed from the bubbling juice. They love it, but they know Charlie is going to kick them away as soon as he sees them. They have sneaked up to the barrel with their tails already between their legs in case they don't see Charlie's kick in time. Sorghum cooking at night is also a social gathering. The children and dogs play games at times and race about in everybody's way. The young men who work as day hands in sawmills and driving trucks come for the social side only. One pair can be seen headed for the bushes with their arms around each other; another pair, seated on the straw-soft pile of pummins, has already been and are back. The moon is new, the horns are up. It is full of water. A ring is around it with two stars in the ring. That means it will rain in forty-eight hours. That's why they are cooking at night. You cannot cook in the rain.

John Faulkner

The House of Doom

In William Faulkner's story "Red Leaves" the Chickasaw chieftain known as Doom is reported to have had a riverboat dragged overland and set up as his residence: "The house sat on a knoll, surrounded by oak trees. The front of it was one story in height, composed of the deck house of a steamboat which had gone ashore and which Doom, Issetibbeha's father, had dismantled with his slaves and hauled on cypress rollers twelve miles home overland. It took them five months. His house consisted at the time of one brick wall. He set the steamboat broadside on to the wall, where now the chipped and flaked gilding of the rococo cornices arched in faint splendor above the gilt lettering of the stateroom names above the jalousied doors."

—William Faulkner, "Red Leaves"

The Legend of a Lake CONTINUED FROM PAGE 23

The fish and their wrecked spawning beds and the rivers of silt and chemicals were set pieces in a gradually enlarging drama. In the primeval days of the lake, about one million algae lived in every quart of water in the western basin. These tiny plants were the genesis, the starting point, for all the lake's life systems. They had undergone delays and diversions in their life cycles during the silt blizzards, but the surface water always clarified enough to allow them to reproduce. In the 1930's they began to proliferate in areas beyond the drifting silt.

They responded to the amount of phosphorus from fertilizers, detergents, and organic sewage flushed into the lake from men's sewers and washed from their artificially managed fields. Within twenty-five years the algae had grown until there were almost four million of them in every quart of water. A special kind of algae, the blue-green, came into dominance. They did not photosynthesize as much oxygen as did the others, but they demanded a greater share of the oxygen at night. The blue-green algae reproduced at high speed, died in enormous numbers, and thus stimulated the omnipresent bacteria waiting for their deaths at the bottom of the lake. The bacteria, themselves now boosted in population, also demanded their share of the oxygen.

The blue-green algae were so well stimulated in their artificially ideal world that they displaced other plants that could not capitalize on the sewer bounty so well. Everywhere they encroached into the territories of the diatoms, suppressed their growth, and so set up a chain reaction that ended with young fish starving to death.

This was a preamble to looming catastrophe. The great submarine meadows of mayfly larvae, which in places consisted of several thousand creatures for every square yard of the lake bottom, were able to thrive through these changing conditions. They remained the great storehouse of food for all bottom-prowling fish. They could live on muddy bottoms. But gradually, oxygen became scarcer and scarcer during summers. The blue-green algae used it, the bacteria needed it; when the lake stratified into layers of different temperatures during hot, calm weather, oxygen at the surface was prevented from circulating to the bottom dwellers. In this stratification the poisonous chemicals from men's works on shore sank to the oxygen-deprived bottom to create a kind of suffocating witch's brew.

In the early suffocations fish fled, and the mayflies and midges died in large numbers; but there were always enough survivors to quickly build up populations again. However, in 1953, with the winds light and the above-water temperatures in the 80's, the depletion of oxygen in the western basin became complete. The loss spread over hundreds of square miles, then thousands. The lake choked, then strangled. Every living creature on the bottom that needed oxygen was killed. The midges were gone. The mayflies, those ancient successes of evolution, were wiped out.

All during the twentieth century the lake demonstrated to the men that before nature could be tamed, nature must be known. But the understanding of such things came slowly to the men. Their ignorance was a shield against the paralyzing verities of the earth. Sometimes they fluked a profit from the lake. In 1940 a group of smelt established themselves in a drainage ditch at the western end of the lake, descendants, perhaps, of sixteen million smelt eggs planted in Lake Michigan in 1912. With dazzling speed they developed in the lake and became, along with the yellow perch, the most common fish there. At least the smelt were edible—unlike the sea lamprey, which had gotten into the upper three Great Lakes and destroyed their trout and other species. The smelt made good cat food, so they might be considered successors to the long-gone ciscoes.

Meanwhile, the yellow walleye that, with the blue pike, had withstood the relentless fishing, changing temperatures, and silt and sewage, quite suddenly went into an inexplicable decline. Both the yellow walleye and the blue pike were each yielding thousands of tons of flesh to fishermen in the mid-1950's. Then, in ten astonishing years, they crashed. The blue pike became too scarce to be worth fishing. The yellow walleye faded to a shadow of its former abundance. This left the yellow perch, which continued to yield good crops of flesh until the 1960's, when it, too, began to decline in number. It spawned amid vegetation, its one great weakness in a lake where rooted plants were having a tough time surviving silt, sewage, and industrial poisons.

The early silt storms had suffocated and smothered, but they did not poison. After an estimated two billion tons of silt had reached the lake from 1850 onward, the silt changed in character. Not only was it laden with phosphates and nitrates—essential chemicals in the works of man—but it also contained hundreds of other chemicals, notably DDT. This last chemical, a few men knew, influenced the hormone estrogen, which, in turn, controlled reproduction in all mammals. DDT could cause mass sterility. Buried in bottom silt, suspended in the water, the DDT was not influenced by any of the water-purifying devices used by the men, who remained faithful to the concept that nature can be mastered. They would "save the lake," as they modestly put it, by building a levee from Ohio to Ontario, turning the western basin of the lake into the world's largest septic tank. They would build a two-mile-long lagoon off the shores of Cleveland and dump its wastes there. They would pump all industrial poisons two thousand feet underground. They would reverse the flow of the Cuyahoga and purify it, and then use the water over and over again.

The plans made noise and headlines, but not much else. When the people of Cleveland could no longer swim on expensive artificial beaches built for them, the beaches were enclosed with plastic, the water killed with chlorine, and the people swam again. But further offshore, a combination of sewage, dead algae, dead fish, industrial rubbish, and untreated flushings from lake freighters sent an awful stench drifting into the streets of downtown Cleveland. Winds hurled the living, dying, and dead algae onto shore, where they smothered miles of beaches, clogged the filters and screens of water-processing plants, and befouled the drinking water of many cities.

The primeval lake had demonstrated an imperative of existence that showed how every living organism had to live in some agreement with the available resources. But for the people of the lake, this imperative was long obsolete. At the city of Erie, in Pennsylvania, the people had turned a seven-mile-long peninsula into a beautiful state park. On summer weekends one hundred thousand of them packed the park and launched twelve thousand power-boats into water loaded with tannins and lignins, stinking with sewage, and foaming with oil wastes.

The people of upstate New York were slightly better off because their drinking water was flavored with the sewage of grape-juice manufacturing. The citizens of Dunkirk, however, were not so lucky; their water included the many flavors of waste taken from color printing, the brown sewage effluents from the production of asphalt, and fly ash dispersed from a power plant. The Buffalo River was so filled with oils, chemicals, and sewage that it was a river of death, lifeless and loathsome. Nevertheless, during heavy rainfalls and dredging, this muck was passed into the people's drinking water intakes. The Cuyahoga River at Cleveland, once the host to the ebullient sturgeon, actually caught fire one day. It burned fiercely and threatened to destroy that city.

By this time the men around the lake faced an Orwellian set of contradictions. Fifty years before, they had not doubted their mastery of nature, but now they had to explain away ten thousand square miles of blundering. It made their science, their technology, look like a maniacal system that had to smash its own house to make progress.

Defensively, they said the lake could be cleaned up, at a cost of billions of dollars. They belatedly began building sewage treatment plants, only to find that mercury, in industrial discharges, was being stored in the bodies of the lake's fish, making them poisonous to eat. Worse, the men seemed unable to stem the flow of silt, the real villain, because it flowed every time a highway was made, a field plowed, a basement dug, a house constructed, a bulldozer blade lowered—acts that were the very heart and soul of civilization's advances. Restoring the lake meant removing all the silt, and that was impossible.

The men had too great an investment in progress based on new engines, new chemicals, new conquests of other worlds to understand relatively simple truths. They understood that the lake was a victim of their works, and they were sorry about that. They could not yet understand that they had become victims of the lake. The state of the lake was also the state of the men.

DUANE MICHAELS

A far cry from the pleasant vista on page 21 is this recent photograph of the Cleveland lakefront. Debris almost hides the water.

OVERLEAF: *Life under the lake's surface, a century ago and today.*

Franklin Russell is a free-lance writer who frequently reports on ecological matters. He is currently working on a book dealing with catastrophes of natural history that have occurred throughout the world.

Fed by clear streams, Lake Erie was the habitat of a wide variety of marine life as recently as a century ago. Both plants and fish thrived, as illustrated by the profusion of fish species on this page. Among them were the smallmouth black bass (1), lake trout (2), carpsucker (3), whitefish (4), black crappie (5), lake sturgeon (6), drum (7), muskellunge (8), yellow walleye (9), sauger (10), channel catfish (11), and blue pike (12). Minnows flit among the larger fish. On the lake bottom, where many fish spawned, is a freshwater mollusk.

The upset in the ecological balance of Lake Erie is reflected in the sparser fish life now found there. Erosion has silted over the spawning grounds on the bottom, which is now also cluttered with refuse. The water itself is clouded by billions of blue-green algae, which proliferate amid the waste discharges from factories and communities. The few fish that have adjusted to the choking conditions include the yellow perch (1), carp (2), smelt (3), goldfish (4), whitesucker (5), brown bullhead (6), white bass (7), and channel catfish (8).

DRAWN BY NICHOLAS FASCIANO

N-X 237
COLUMBIA

How Not to Fly the Atlantic CONTINUED FROM PAGE 47

the liner, banked, and came back right over the ship and along her wake. This invisible air path would lead him to Land's End.

Half an hour after leaving the *Mauretania* Chamberlin sighted the *Memphis*, which was bringing Lindbergh home. But she was about ten miles to the south, and he turned down Levine's suggestion that they fly over and "jazz her up" a bit. The afternoon was waning and so was the perfect weather. A haze dead ahead was thickening, low hanging clouds had appeared, and flashes of lightning heralded rain squalls.

Before sunset they saw other ships, and at last, through the haze, they saw the low cliffs of Land's End, lighted by the long rays of the setting sun.

The wind behind them had strengthened; and while their air path over the sea was smooth, it became turbulent over the land. They circled above the coast, checking its outlines with their charts. Dusk was moving in over the green countryside. With a black, stormy night in prospect there was a great temptation to land on the hospitable Cornish shore.

Now the clouds were becoming thick. Chamberlin climbed above them and headed eastward. Through a rift in the rack he saw Plymouth and got another bearing. In distance they were about five hours' flying time from Berlin. But the clouds were rising higher. Chamberlin realized he was very tired, that he might not be able to find the German capital, and that even if he did, he might have trouble landing there in the dark. He headed in the direction of Berlin but decided that if he reached it, he would stay aloft till dawn. There was plenty of gas to last through the short night.

The Bellanca had climbed to fifteen thousand feet. With the cloud mass still rising in the east, the plane had to go higher. Chamberlin nursed it up to eighteen thousand, then twenty thousand feet. Still the cloud barrier to the east towered above them.

Should they try to fly through it? They might hit a mountain although their altimeter showed they had plenty of altitude. The only thing to do, Chamberlin felt, was to fly along the western side of the cloud range and kill time till he had enough light to see if it extended all the way down to the earth.

So he flew north for fifteen minutes, then turned and flew south for another fifteen, repeating the turnabout over and over until he realized he was nearing exhaustion. The thin air was making the plane hard to handle. He had to work the controls almost continually to keep the machine level. And insufficient oxygen, added to forty hours of sleeplessness, was making him lightheaded.

Dawn paled the east again, and Chamberlin was sure he would pass out soon unless he got a little rest. They were still flying at twenty thousand feet or higher, with the cloud floor visible below them. Surely Levine could handle the ship for a while.

"See what you can do with her," Chamberlin told his companion. And he moved back in the plane and stretched out on the gas-tank shelf. Levine kept the plane level for about ten minutes. But in the thin air the machine was hard to control.

In some way, either by losing altitude or by following a canyon in the clouds, he got into the bewildering mist. Then, as inexperienced pilots sometimes do, he tried so hard to keep the plane horizontal that he pulled the nose up too far and the Bellanca stalled. Unable to rise higher, it pointed its left wing toward the earth and went into a deadly spiral. Levine, unable to see anything but mist, had no idea what was happening.

But Chamberlin, half asleep, sensed disaster. He slid off the tank and into his seat. The Bellanca's wings had started to shiver. The rudder was flapping violently back and forth, shaking the rear end of the plane as if it would tear it off. It was also whipping the rudder bar to and fro so viciously that Chamberlin didn't dare to try to stop it all at once.

Understanding their danger, Chamberlin was badly scared, but Levine seemed to enjoy the situation. He had taken his hand off the quivering stick and his feet off the jerking rudder bar and was sitting there chuckling at the antics of the plane. It was behaving, he said later, like a bucking bronco.

These antics, the rush of air, and the instruments told Chamberlin that they were headed toward the ground at terrifying speed. The altimeter needle was racing past hundred-foot marks as if they represented inches. The needle on the air-speed indicator was jammed against the pin that marked 160 miles an hour, the most the instrument was capable of showing.

Chamberlin knew that if he tried to pull out too suddenly he probably would rip the wings off the plane; that if he pushed too hard against the rudder bar it would break the control cables. He set about the second task gingerly, pushing at the bar with increasing strength as it neared the end of its swing. Gradually he tamed the berserk bar and was able to steer out of the spiral. Then he slowly flattened the dive till the plane lost its

Near Klinge, unplanned stop Number Two on the way to Berlin, Chamberlin and Levine stand by the tail of their rugged little plane. Its propeller was broken in landing on a soggy pasture.

dangerous speed.

By this time the altimeter showed four thousand feet. They had dropped more than three miles. Still they were in the gray mist. All they could see through the windshield were the blue spurts from the Whirlwind's exhaust pipes. The flames turned the haze into an eerie blue blur.

Chamberlin figured they were somewhere over Germany. He knew that the Harz Mountains were several thousand feet high and thought they must be somewhere near. Nevertheless he decided to go lower and try to find some landmark shown on their chart. They slid down below a thousand feet before they came out of the gray to find themselves flying in rain over a river. Soon they saw the glare of blast furnaces. Chamberlin thought they must be over Essen. Levine disagreed. He said the lights below were those of Bremerhaven. As proof, he added that he had been in Bremerhaven once.

They flew around in the rain, looking for a name on a factory roof. From the air the scene was like the traditional concept of hell. Flames flared up from the blast furnaces, painting the low clouds a lurid red. Even if they had wanted to land in the area, it probably would have been impossible in that storm. They didn't know till next day that the city was Dortmund.

Soon they saw white flares being fired into the air not far away. They headed toward them and saw a flying field. On it, in the growing light, they could make out some figures. Chamberlin idled the engine, came down to about twenty feet, stuck his hand out the window, and yelled down at the top of his voice to the men on the ground, "*Nach Berlin? Nach Berlin?*" He swept over their heads and banked around to see if they had understood him. All of them pointed in about the same direction. Chamberlin headed that way.

It was now shortly after 4:30 A.M. Their fuel was getting low. They were actually pointing eastward from Dortmund on a course that would take them south of the German capital; but both men thought they were heading for Berlin, and Chamberlin held the course till the gasoline gauge neared zero.

He wanted to land near some large village while he still had some fuel left and could use the engine in landing. But Levine insisted on going on till the last drop was used. So Chamberlin told him to go to the rear of the cabin and act as ballast, for with empty tanks the Bellanca was nose heavy. A few minutes later the faithful engine coughed and stopped. Chamberlin brought the plane into the wind and came down in a pretty, dead-stick landing. Shortly before six o'clock the Bellanca rolled to a smooth halt in a small wheat field near the town of Eisleben.

They had been in the air for forty-three hours and were still 110 miles short of Berlin, though their straight-line distance from Roosevelt Field was 3,905 miles—295 longer than Lindbergh's. Actually their zigzag course had taken them well over four thousand miles. Indeed, Chamberlin estimated later that in the last ten hours of their journey they had moved eastward only three hundred miles, though they must have flown a thousand in that time.

They had come down safely, however, and there was plenty of reason to be thankful. In the sudden silence they heard the singing of birds. Gratefully they got out of the plane and stretched their stiff limbs. Chamberlin found he couldn't stand upright unless he kept moving. When he stood still he swayed drunkenly.

Nobody was in sight. Nearly half an hour passed. The bird song was beginning to pall. Then a woman with two boys crossed the field and came up to them. She spoke to the two men in German, apparently complaining about the wheat they had smashed. Chamberlin replied with the few phrases he remembered from his high-school German. Then Levine tried. Suddenly the anger on the woman's face gave way to fear. She spoke urgently to the boys, and all three turned and ran. Long afterward Chamberlin learned that she had taken them for some kidnapers who had been terrorizing the area.

Other field workers appeared. Within an hour a small group of men, women, and children were looking curiously at the strangers and the plane. They didn't seem to believe that the two men were "*von New York gekommen*"; but they finally comprehended that the *Columbia* needed fuel, and one of the boys volunteered to bicycle four miles and arrange for ninety liters of benzol to be sent to the field. Chamberlin wanted to ask him to fetch a map, too, but he couldn't think of the German word.

After an hour a truck appeared with the benzol—twenty-two gallons of it. It wasn't gasoline, but the Whirlwind would run on it. However, the truck driver's funnel was too big to use on the cabin tank, and the wing tanks had been sealed to make any distance flight official. Obligingly, one of the women walked a mile across the fields and came back with a long-necked teapot. It took Chamberlin an hour and a half and a hundred trips back and forth with the teapot to feed the benzol into the *Columbia*'s gas tank.

A boy who spoke fair English appeared to act as translator. He told them they could get a map in Eisleben, but as everybody agreed that Berlin was "that way," the fliers decided to start without it. Unfortunately, they had left the inertia starter behind because of its weight. And Chamberlin was so weak he could hardly stand up.

A fellow who said he was an airplane mechanic offered to throw the propeller over by hand, but he proved to be so awkward that Chamberlin feared the man would be killed if the engine started. So the weary pilot himself hauled the blades around. With Levine manipulating the switch and throttle he toiled for half an hour—yelling "Contact!" and "Switch off!" time and again—before the Whirlwind took hold and began to roar.

The farm people held the wheel struts and tail skid while Chamberlin tested the engine with its new fuel. It seemed to be all right, and he signalled them to stand clear. Then he opened the throttle. The field was damp but not soggy, and the *Columbia* rose from it easily. It circled around the field and headed for Berlin, or at least in the direction the farm workers seemed to have pointed.

But exactly how had they pointed? The two men couldn't agree. Levine thought they ought to bear more to the northeast, Chamberlin more to the east. The weather was clear, and Levine was now flying the ship some of the time. When he had the controls, they went northeast. When Chamberlin had them, they went east. It was one of the few times that Levine was right.

They should have reached Berlin in an hour. But after ninety minutes they saw only a small city with the name COTTBUS marked on its flying field. A map would have shown them they were already past Berlin and about seventy miles south of it. They flew on for about twenty-five miles. The country under them was getting swampy; the benzol was almost gone. Chamberlin banked around and headed back toward the Cottbus airfield.

Five miles short of it the engine stopped. Levine got behind the gas tank, using his weight as ballast again, but this time the landing place was a soggy pasture. As the plane rolled more slowly, one of the wheels sank in to the hub. The *Columbia* stood up on its nose, and the walnut-wood propeller, which had stopped in an up-and-down position, snapped off at the bottom. Every loose object in the cabin surged forward. Powdered milk and chocolate, parts of their emergency rations, cascaded down on Chamberlin, giving his head and shoulders a chocolate-milk-shake hue.

It was now about 11:30 A.M. As the two men slid out of the up-tilted plane, a peasant woman ran up and began to jabber at them in German. Pointing to the wheel ruts the *Columbia* had made in the field, she screamed "Pay! Pay!" (*"Bezahlen! Bezahlen!"*) A crowd quickly gathered around them.

They had come down near the village of Klinge, whose burgomaster soon arrived to welcome them. Apparently the *Columbia*'s presence in Germany was now well-known. But before the burgomaster could drive them into Klinge, Burgomaster Kreutz, of Cottbus, drove up. Frowning terribly at his fellow mayor, he told the fliers it was a frightful mistake about Klinge. They had really landed at Cottbus, a town capable of giving them appropriate entertainment. Soon he had shoved his feebly protesting rival from Klinge into the background.

When the *Columbia* was eased down to its tail skid, Burgomaster Kreutz assigned two Cottbus policemen to keep off souvenir hunters and then whisked the Americans into town. At the Hotel Ansorges, the best hostelry Cottbus afforded, he plied them with crab soup, fried eels, roast goose, and beer. While they were eating, fifteen planes from Berlin arrived, eight of them carrying newspapermen and photographers. Cheering citizens of Cottbus massed outside the hotel, many of them to remain there till late at night.

Lufthansa offered to fly the Americans into Berlin. But both wanted to arrive there in the *Columbia*. In the afternoon Chamberlin went back to the plane and asked that it be towed to a nearby soccer field. He also asked for a new propeller and some gasoline.

The Lufthansa men were amazed at the small size of the Bellanca. Beside some of the German planes it looked like a toy. But they were positive that, small as it was, it couldn't take off from a regulation soccer field. They wanted to dismantle the machine, take the parts to the Cottbus airport, and reassemble it there. Chamberlin finally convinced them he knew what he was talking about, and they had the plane towed to the drier ground. They also wired for a propeller to be taken from an experimental Heinkel plane that was fitted with two Whirlwind engines.

Back at the hotel, Levine, basking in his sudden fame, was talking volubly to newspapermen while the hastily assembled Cottbus band serenaded him from the street. At his very first press conference on German soil Levine was inadvertently emphasizing the difference that can exist between heroes.

Lindbergh had done everything right. He had made a magnificent flight—alone—to his announced destination and had arrived there on schedule. Thereafter he had been modest, generous, and gracious. He had made his first call in Paris on the mother of Charles Nungesser, one of the fliers lost while trying to make the transatlantic flight a few weeks earlier. Lindbergh had told her how much he admired her son and had expressed hope that the famous French ace might yet be found. He had taken 150,000 francs (then worth about $5,850) that a French aeronautic club had awarded to him and donated it to swell a fund for families of lost French fliers. He had turned down a million-dollar purse that some Americans wanted to raise for him. And he had refrained from publicly criticizing his transatlantic rivals and from disparaging their often questionable activities.

The *Columbia* group's performance—thanks largely to Levine—had been a comedy of errors for months. He had battled with associates, schemed, lied, and nearly killed himself and Chamberlin in a fatal spin. Yet in spite of everything—thanks largely to Chamberlin—the *Columbia* had crossed the Atlantic. Now Levine was close to exhaustion after eighty hours without sleep and from the excitement and alarms of the journey. Characteristically, however, he was still able to say the wrong thing. "We've made a record even if we haven't reached Berlin," he told the first American newspaperman who got to him. "Believe me, if we had had Lindbergh's luck we would have reached Berlin with enough gasoline for three or four hundred miles more." Then he added, with a grin, "We had plenty of luck, only it was all hard."

When Chamberlin returned from the field, they had a big dinner and after that eased themselves into hot tubs. Then, oblivious to the booming of the band outside the hotel, they slipped into bed and sleep. Lincoln Eyre, of the *New York Times*, who had flown down to Cottbus to greet them, wrote that their sleep was sound and happy because they had carried through to completion "one of the most splendid enterprises ever achieved by man on land, or sea or in the air."

The next day, everybody agreed, was the greatest in the 997-year history of Cottbus. Outside the Hotel Ansorges people massed on all sides of the square. The Americans emerged from the building to a tremendous ovation from the crowd. "*Hoch! Hoch!*" the admiring townspeople shouted. Then the airmen rode in state to the town hall, where they signed the guest book, whose pages are opened only to distinguished visitors. The old building's reception hall was bursting with still more people, who cheered them from the floor and from the galleries. On the wall above the rostrum hung a new flag, made during the night. It had thirty stars and no stripes, but its colors were red, white, and blue.

Burgomaster Kreutz led the heroes to seats on the rostrum. "Has the music arrived?" he asked an aide. The music had, and the band, which provided it, had been working—like the flag makers—far into the night. It burst into a rendition of "The Star-Spangled Banner" with an enthusiasm that almost drowned out the mistakes.

The burgomaster made a speech of welcome and praise. Then the counselor of the American Embassy, who had flown down from Berlin, read a speech of acknowledgment in German. After that the band again broke into its version of "The Star-Spangled Banner," and everybody stood up in the anthem's honor.

Now Burgomaster Kreutz presented the visitors with two splendid silver salvers and made them honorary citizens of Cottbus. This meant, he explained, that they could return to the city and live there rent free for the rest of their lives.

The band was so pleased with its performance to date that it now attempted to play "The Star-Spangled Banner" a third time. But the burgomaster shushed it before the assembly could rise again. Several other dignitaries made speeches, and the ceremony ended with "Deutschland über Alles," which the Germans sang with great enthusiasm and considerable volume.

The crowd outside the town hall gave the visitors another big hand, and two little girls curtsied and presented them with bouquets. Then they drove to the soccer field, where Lufthansa mechanics had replaced the broken propeller and put some gasoline in the *Columbia*'s tanks.

Chamberlin found that the new prop, which was larger and more sharply pitched than the other, would turn at only 1,350 revolutions a minute, three hundred less than its predecessor. He wasn't sure how well it would work, so he left Levine to proceed by car. The Lufthansa men, who were sure he couldn't take off in such a small area, were amazed when he used hardly a third of the available space. He flew to Cottbus in about three minutes. At the White Horse Hotel there he and Levine were luncheon guests of Burgomaster Kreutz.

All this time, plans for the *official* reception in Berlin were under way. The dignitaries in Berlin wanted the Tempelhof ceremony to start at 6 P.M. And so fearful was Burgomaster Kreutz that they might be late for it that he got the fliers started from the Cottbus airport at 4:30 for the seventy-mile flight to the capital. This time the Americans had an escort of fifteen planes, so they could hardly get lost. In fact, they reached Berlin ahead of schedule and had to circle over the city for twenty minutes before the welcoming committee was ready. ☆

WIDE WORLD

Although Levine never paid Chamberlin $15,000 of the $25,000 promised for the Columbia *flight, the two men seemed amiable when they met in 1962 at a reunion of the Long Island Early Flying Club. Chamberlin now sells real estate in Connecticut; Levine, after various brushes with the law, has dropped from sight.*

"Mad Jack" and the Missionaries CONTINUED FROM PAGE 37

After several unsuccessful attempts to trick *Dolphin*'s midshipmen into giving up his specie, Edwards finally agreed to have the salvage fee deducted and took the remainder on board *Becket*, preparatory to sailing on March 13. Edwards told Percival he expected to sue on his return to the United States, but Percival merely shrugged and answered: "I'm not worth $500 anyway, and I would as lief die in jail as in a drawing room."

But Edwards had one more arrow in his quiver. He had his steward spread a report on shore that Percival had stolen one of *London*'s mattresses. He expected to be at sea before the scurrilous story reached Mad Jack's ears, but he was not so fortunate; for as *Becket* was being towed out of the harbor, Edwards saw Percival leave the beach in a whaleboat and go on board *Dolphin*. A few minutes later another boat left *Dolphin*, containing Percival and Paulding in addition to the boat's crew, and very shortly Edwards found himself facing an angry John Percival on *Becket*'s quarter-deck. A heated exchange followed, until finally Mad Jack roared: "You told your steward to look in my room for a mattress belonging to you, and you must go on shore and deny it!"

"No, I won't," returned Edwards.

"Then I'll thrash you!" exploded Mad Jack, and seizing Edwards by the collar with his left hand, Percival spun him around, knocked off his hat, and beat him sharply about the head and shoulders with his stout whalebone cane. The two men fell scuffling to the deck, but Edwards soon regained his feet and ran forward to the fife rail, where he began seizing belaying pins and stanchions and hurling them. Than he picked up an axe. "Put it down, Edwards," cried Percival. "You dare as well go to hell as strike me with that!" Edwards said he would strike but on second thought laid down the axe and picked up a gun rammer. This he struck against something a few times to knock off the sponge, but failing, he aimed a blow at Percival from well out of range. The sponge flew off and whistled by Percival's ear; after Edwards swung the rammer a few more times Percival, seeing that Edwards was afraid to come near enough to hit him, called to some of the boat's crew who had slipped on deck: "Grab the damned rascal and take that thing away from him!" Three or four men separated Edwards from the rammer, and Percival told them to let him go; Edwards darted down the companionway to his cabin.

After Percival returned to *Dolphin*, *Becket* got under way, bearing Edwards and his rancor against Mad Jack Percival home to America. In the evening, Captain McNeill of *Convoy*, doubtless pleased at having received his charter money at last—Percival had paid it out of the salvage charges—gave a dinner on board for *Dolphin*'s officers.

The merchant and whaling community for the most part was well pleased with Mad Jack. Percival had brought pressure on the chiefs to pay their debts to the traders and had persuaded Boki and the captains of the trading and whaling ships to agree to port regulations that, by requiring captains to pay a fine of six dollars for any of their men who deserted at Honolulu, were designed to reduce the community of penniless desperadoes that had furnished the instigators of the *Globe* mutiny. The captains of the whaling ships were so pleased with Percival, in fact, that they signed a circular letter asking him to stay at Honolulu as long as possible. These ships represented a trade of substantial proportions: a contemporary estimate placed the value of the ships and cargoes visiting Honolulu between February 1 and May 1, 1826, at more than two million dollars.

Early in April the American consul at the islands, John Coffin Jones, returned from a visit to the United States. Jones doubled as agent for Marshall and Wildes and represented the traders' point of view. He soon wrote to both his employers—Josiah Marshall on the one hand, Secretary of State Henry Clay on the other—that *Dolphin* had performed "essential service to American concerns in this place." Jones and Percival saw eye to eye on the missionary question; as Jones told Marshall:

> The missionaries have succeeded in frightening these poor simple children of nature into the belief of a religion they do not understand themselves, the very need of which is a libel on the goodness of God. The distress of the Country, the distracted state of the government and the wretchedness which on every

HAWAIIAN MISSION CHILDREN'S SOCIETY, HONOLULU

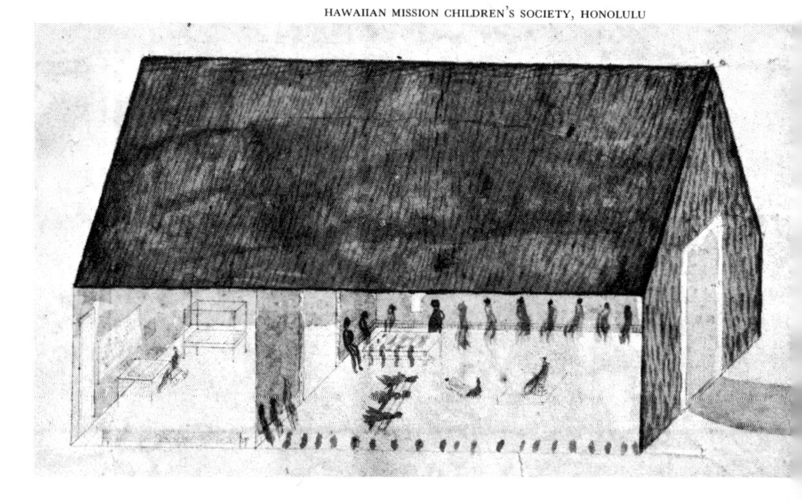

The first mission school in Honolulu, an austere two-room house drawn here by G. Holmes in 1821, was run by Sybil Bingham.

side stare you in the face (all caused by the hypocritical emissaries sent here from the work shop of their sect) would beggar were I to attempt a description. Nothing but the sound of the church going bell is heard from the rising to the setting sun and religion is crammed down the throats of these poor, simple mortals. . . .

There was, however, one merchant whom Percival could not win over—Stephen Reynolds. Part of the difficulty seems to have been that Reynolds was a friend of Edwards, and also of Leonard Sistare, the charming master of the American merchant schooner *Adonis*, who had decamped with his ship, counting on losing himself in the islands and living on the proceeds of *Adonis* and her cargo. Sistare had been understandably chagrined, therefore, when Percival arrived with orders for his arrest, and his friend Reynolds shared his displeasure. (Apparently Percival solved the problem by impounding Sistare's strongbox, leaving the culprit himself at the islands.) Another factor in the Percival-Reynolds quarrel may have been simply that Reynolds was, as his diary reveals, a man who liked no one for very long. At any rate, Sistare reported to Reynolds that Percival had accused him of going to Reynolds' house to consult with "Old Pierpoint Edwards, a bald-headed old rascal. I gave him a good caneing, the damned rascal!" Three days later Reynolds recorded that two female natives had told him that Percival advised them to trade at the wooden house, rather than at Reynolds' store. "Many other things were told me showing him to be the basest, meanest of men I have ever known."

Reynolds was therefore prepared to record with the utmost glee the vicissitudes of Percival's adventures with the native women. One night, while lodging at Captain Grimes's house, Percival received a tin-pan serenade from some sailors and merchants—something akin to a "shivaree" on the frontier back home. Whether this incident frightened his native "wife" or whether there were other concubinal difficulties is not clear, but on March 19 Reynolds noted a "report" that Percival had "got Black Jo [a Portuguese *bravo*, or desperado, who resided on Oahu] to go with him to Gov. Boki to demand a young girl who Hero [Percival] fear[s] had run away from him. Boki gave the word and she was sent to him!!!" The next day, as Captain Peleg Stetson of the whaler *Phoenix* later recalled, Percival had some guests at his house; he pointed to his bed and observed to Stetson that the girl who shared it with him had run away but had been returned by Boki. In Reynolds' version, however, Percival had described "his treatment [of] a young girl—too disgraceful to be related."

Percival had intended to leave the islands early in April, but the petitions of the whaling captains and the

BOTH: BERNICE P. BISHOP MUSEUM, HONOLULU

With the dowager queen Kaahumanu seated in attendance, Hiram Bingham preaches to a group of Hawaiians at Waimea, Oahu, in 1826. This woodcut was made after a sketch drawn by Bingham himself. The original caption says he is "recommending Christianity" to them.

persuasion of Consul Jones induced him to stay a few weeks longer. Commodore Hull was already anxious about *Dolphin;* having fitted her in August for a six months' cruise, he had expected her back at Callao by January or February. At last, on the morning of May 11, 1826, *Dolphin* weighed anchor, exchanged salutes with the fort, and stood out of Honolulu Harbor. She reached Callao on August 24 after a cruise of more than a year. At Oahu she left fond memories in the minds of the trading community and of the whalemen, and rancor in the hearts of the missionaries.

Bingham's enmity, and that of Edwards, pursued Percival to America, where he was subjected to a court of inquiry in 1828 on charges of unofficerlike and ungentlemanly conduct toward Edwards, of opposing morality at the islands, and of personal lewdness. However, the court, composed of three captains, decided that the evidence against Percival was not sufficient to warrant a court-martial. Subsequently Percival made a cruise on the Brazil station, then sailed under Hull once more as commander of the new sloop of war *Cyane* in the Mediterranean. By then (1838–39) Percival was afflicted with gout, which made him "snappish as a bear with a sore head," according to one midshipman. He was sometimes heard soliloquizing in his cabin to the effect that he would probably not live to return to America. He did; but his apprehension perhaps accounts for the fact that on his last voyage in 1844 he carried an oak coffin in his cabin. This cruise took Percival around the world in the frigate *Constitution.* Returning to America for the last time in 1846, Mad Jack installed the unused coffin as a watering trough at his home in Dorchester, Massachusetts, where he died September 17, 1862, at age eighty-three.

Although Percival's conduct in Hawaii had drawn no reproach from the government, the pens and press of the missionaries fastened the stigma of bad conduct on him. Measures for the collection of debts, for regulating the conduct of seamen at Honolulu, for preventing desertion, and for rendering aid to *London* and other vessels in distress were all forgotten in favor of Bingham's facile characterization of *Dolphin* as "the mischief-making man of war." Nevertheless Master Commandant Thomas ap Catesby Jones, who visited Honolulu in *Peacock* a few months after Percival had left, credited his predecessor for the good order he found among the shipping there. And it is surely to the credit of Mad Jack and his crew that the bloody mutiny aboard *Globe* was the last in the annals of American Pacific whaling.

Mrs. McKee, who holds a Ph.D. in American studies, was Visiting Research Associate in Naval History at the Smithsonian Institution last year.

Despite the missionaries' campaign to ban such agreeable diversions, luaus with native dancing continued for many years in Hawaii. This festive party, for officers of the French corvette La Bonite, *was held in 1836 and drawn by a member of* La Bonite*'s crew named Lauvergne.*

The Fight for the Queen . . . CONTINUED FROM PAGE 7

itation are almost invisible for miles. Occasionally a road or railroad line appears between towns, and the *Queen*, on this last trip, got a blast of friendship now and then from a long freight train or honking horns from massed lines of cars parked at some high point to see history go by. The crowds were thick at the locks of the upper river;

OLIVER JENSEN

As the Queen *sinks into a lock on her "last trip," President William Muster addresses a sympathetic crowd from the bridge.*

you get a very close look there, and the Army engineers have built scores of these locks. Great, impressive affairs they are for controlling floods and making navigation easy. Indeed, they seem to have reached a kind of apogee of usefulness and efficiency just in time for the last passengers. Mark Twain, a man with a pretty good sense of irony and a gift of prophecy, put these words into the mouth of the mate of a riverboat back in 1882:

> Government is doing a deal for the Mississippi now, spending loads of money on her. When there used to be four thousand steamboats and ten thousand acres of coal barges, and rafts, and trading scows, there wasn't a lantern from St. Paul to New Orleans, and now, when there's three dozen steamboats and nary a barge or raft, government has snatched out all the snags, and lit up the shores like Broadway, and a boat's as safe on the river as she'd be in heaven. And I reckon that by the time there *ain't any boats left at all*, the Commission will have the old thing all *reorganized*, and *dredged out*, and *fenced in*, and *tidied up*, to a degree that will make navigation just *simply perfect*, and *absolutely* safe and profitable.

As the *Queen* dropped into the great lock at Keokuk, Twain's comments seemed apt enough. The works are a marvelous achievement and, from any human standpoint, perfectly useless hereafter unless you are a barge load of coal.

So it went all during this last trip, visitors streaming aboard wherever possible for a last look at the gleaming brass, broad stairways, and the rest of the old-fashioned elegance, passengers glumly contemplating the banks when not diverted by good food, music, and entertainment—all of this in strange counterpoint to the sense of gloom. At Vicksburg the reception was so warm and tearful, the captain jested, that the Yazoo River rose half a foot. Officials of the venerable Greene Line, which operates the *Delta Queen*, estimated that as many as a quarter of a million people had written their congressmen or signed petitions to keep her on the rivers. Editorial writers mourned her passing all through the Middle West.

Why, with all this support and affection, was the old steamboat in danger? This, as anyone interested in historic preservation will recognize, is a silly question; it takes us back to Washington, where riverboats and sentiment are normally no match for lethargy, bureaucracy, and vested interests. The sword that hung over the *Queen*'s head is called Public Law 89–777, or, more popularly if not so accurately, the Safety at Sea Act of 1966. It was passed after a disastrous fire on the S.S. *Yarmouth Castle* in the Caribbean, during which ninety lives were lost. Hereafter, the Coast Guard had decided, there would be no wood at all in vessels flying the American flag if they carried fifty passengers or more in overnight or longer passage. (The lives of forty-nine or fewer overnighters, apparently, do not concern anyone, and daytime travellers seem to be on their own.) There would be no exceptions, for bureaucracy hates exceptions, even for a riverboat that can always be beached in less than five minutes.

Although she has a steel hull, the upper works of the *Delta Queen* are indeed of wood. That fire-retardant paints have been used; that every room and space has sprinklers (just as in the new *Queen Elizabeth* II); that she has passed every inspection; that the fire underwriters are satisfied with her hydrants, pumps, warning systems, and all the other precautions; that the Greene Line, after eighty years in business with twenty-eight ships, has never lost a passenger—none of this seemed to make a difference.

The *Yarmouth Castle*, as President William Muster of the Greene Line was quick to point out, had been recently remodelled in 1965 to Coast Guard specifications of the time, which dictated that sprinklers need be installed only in passenger spaces. Yet the fire began in an unprotected storeroom and thus got beyond control. The Coast Guard ridiculed the business of simply beaching the

Queen in case of fire by citing the tragic fire in 1904 on the New York excursion steamer *General Slocum*, which cost about a thousand lives. She had been beached, hadn't she? But the staff work behind the Coast Guard argument was sketchy: it failed to mention that the *Slocum* was a deep-water boat, whose bow went high on beaching, unlike a flat-bottomed river steamer, which is built to nose up to shore on an even keel as a regular procedure. But most importantly, the *Slocum* had fatally postponed seeking the beach and foolishly steamed on into the wind for many agonizing minutes, which only spread the flames on the overcrowded decks. To make matters worse, the crew was inept, the life preservers and hoses had rotted, pumps had failed to work, lifeboats were wired down, and there had been no fire precautions at all.

So went the argument; this and much more. But the problem for the *Delta Queen*, whose time would soon run out, was neither the sentimental nor the common-sense arguments for saving her. Legislators who had written the 1966 law made plain that they had meant it for salt-water vessels, not riverboats. The Senate passed three bills to exempt the *Delta Queen*, two unanimously, one by 68 to 1. The Department of the Interior, only four months before the *Queen*'s operating life would expire on November 2, placed her on the National Register of historic landmarks that should be preserved. What stopped the wheel and stilled the whistle of the *Queen* was that remarkable instrument of absolutism, the committee system of the United States House of Representatives, a supposedly democratic institution that can be in fact about as responsive to the public will as the Politburo or the court of Louis XVI. Perhaps a little less.

The committee concerned with the *Queen* was that on Merchant Marine and Fisheries, presided over by the somewhat strange figure of Edward A. Garmatz, a representative from Maryland. Elevated to his imperial powers over matters maritime by the inexorable House rules of seniority, Chairman Garmatz is not only the congressional echo of the Coast Guard but the voice of the shipping industry and its powerful unions, for whom, in carefully watered and tended maritime bills, he obtains the annual subsidies amounting to half or more of the annual outlays for our fast-vanishing merchant fleet. It no doubt irritated Congressman Garmatz last fall when the *New York Times* printed an account of how he had accepted thirty-seven thousand dollars from his shipping friends as "campaign contributions," even though he was unopposed in both the primary and the November election itself. And about the same time it clearly infuriated him to have a Senate amendment that would spare the *Delta Queen* tacked on to his omnibus maritime bill. He killed the amendment in committee, as only a chairman can, knowing it would pass if he ever permitted it to reach the floor of the House. In fact, twenty-five *Delta Queen* bills, all dutifully referred to the Merchant Marine Committee, disappeared in similar fashion, *spurlos versenkt*, in his dusty pigeonholes. His prestige was at stake; he had taken his position. The Greene Line should build a new, all-steel riverboat, he said; he had even given them extensions of time to do so. The price, when the line despairingly sought bids among American shipbuilders, was a preposterous ten million dollars; shopping among the congressman's industrial welfare clients is not for bargain hunters.*

Yet democracy does have its occasional day in court, even in Washington, although its ends must sometimes be achieved by means as furtive as those employed by the opposition. The friends of the *Queen* in the Senate quietly added a three-year extension of her life to a private bill (it reimbursed a postal employee for his moving expenses), passed it, and sent it, in a kind of end run, to the House Judiciary Committee, thus evading Mr. Garmatz. There Congressman William M. McCulloch, of Ohio, ranking minority Republican on the Judiciary Committee, shepherded it at length to the floor for debate—a rare thing indeed for a private bill. It was all over in an hour, with a vote of 295 to 73 to give the *Queen* three more years. The last-minute outcries of Congressman Garmatz, who warned of "blood" and disaster and quoted his Coast Guard sources, lost some of their conviction in the face of the headlines of the moment. Just a few days before the vote the Coast Guard, in its most bureaucratic and shameful hour, had returned the now famous Lithuanian defector to his Soviet tormentors.

Most congressmen, if given the chance, would have made the exemption permanent; indeed, so the Senate originally voted. But "getting the chance" is the heart of the matter. Getting to a vote is the great defect of our slow-moving institutions; it is the problem that over and over again faces those who, like the friends of the *Delta Queen*, like all lovers of historic preservation, like (we suspect) most readers of this magazine and certainly its staff, strive to save what is good in past and present from the mindless forces of supergovernment, superlabor, superindustry, and the faceless future. And so, finishing our instructive tale, we must note that the battle will come up again in three years, that Mark Twain's prophecy may still come totally true, that there will almost certainly be another last trip down the great river of the West, and another mad delay—and what will the outcome be? *O navis!* ☆

*On the same specifications a Dutch shipyard bid only four million, but another handy U.S. maritime law, the Jones Act, stipulates that American-flag vessels of any great size must be built in the United States.

The "Mostest Hoss"

CONTINUED FROM PAGE 29

did the bloodlines of Man o' War's sire, Fair Play, and his dam, who had been sired by the great English stallion Rock Sand, winner in 1903 of the 2,000 Guineas, the Epsom Derby, and the St. Leger—Great Britain's Triple Crown.

On the male side of his pedigree, Man o' War was fifteen generations removed from the Godolphin Arabian (born circa 1724), one of the three Arab and Barb stallions that the British consider the founders of the thoroughbred line. On his dam's side, Man o' War traced back to the Layton Barb mare, one of the forty-odd foundation mares of the thoroughbred line.

Fair Play was a first-class animal capable of carrying high weight over a distance, but he was hampered by a fractious temperament inherited from his sire, Hastings. During a race, Hastings would try to slam into other horses and savage them with his teeth as he raced by. He was no less vicious with humans, and he went to his death unreconstructed and unloved, having left his mark literally and figuratively on many a stablehand.

Man o' War's dam, Mahubah, on the other hand, was a big, rangy mare with a sweet disposition that she inherited from her father, Rock Sand, whom Belmont imported in 1908 for the then-record price of $125,000.

Mr. Belmont, then, got what he hoped for from the Fair Play-Rock Sand "cross": a big, powerful animal capable of running a distance under heavy weight with the speed of a sprinter; a colt with the fire of Fair Play and Hastings, tempered by the intelligence and gentleness of Mahubah and Rock Sand. A dream horse.

The United States entered the First World War one week after Big Red was foaled, and Belmont, though sixty-five years old, volunteered. He was commissioned a major and sent to France, where one of his duties was the procurement of mules for the Army. Thus preoccupied, Belmont decided to sell his entire 1917 yearling crop with the exception of Big Red, whom his wife had originally named My Man o' War in his honor, later dropping the "My." At the last minute, however, Belmont changed his mind and cabled instructions to include Man o' War in the consignment to the Saratoga Yearling Sales.

The twenty-one Belmont yearlings were to go under the hammer on August 17, 1918. A few days before the sale Sam Riddle went from stall to stall, looking them over carefully. In the last stall he saw a big chestnut colt that caught his eye, and he asked the groom to lead him outside where he could get a better look at him. It was Man o' War. Riddle later recalled: "[As] soon as I saw him in the daylight he simply bowled me over. . . . I couldn't think of anything but that colt after that. . . ."

In 1918 Riddle was a newcomer to big-time racing, having campaigned only a few middling horses. He had acquired trainer Louis Feustel from Belmont's entourage and had come to Saratoga with his checkbook to build the nucleus of a racing stable. He wound up buying eleven yearlings for a total of $25,000.

A certain amount of resentment and jealousy attended Riddle's good fortune in acquiring Man o' War. A man approaching sixty, Riddle had about him the air of the full-time gentleman-sportsman; he could be pompous and blustery on occasion. But there's a saying in the horse business that the expert is the man who is right

WIDE WORLD

In the last outing of his career, Man o' War handily defeated the English Triple Crown champion Sir Barton in a match race at Kenilworth Park, Windsor, Canada. With Clarence Kummer up, he finished the mile and a quarter seven lengths in front of Sir Barton.

once, and Riddle knew a good horse when he saw one. Furthermore, Man o' War's best interests always came first with him, and that is why Big Red did not compete in 1920 for what later became institutionalized, through publicity, as the tempting American Triple Crown—the Kentucky Derby, the Preakness, and the Belmont Stakes. It was Riddle's belief that early May was too soon in the year to ask a soft-boned three-year-old to run a mile and one quarter, so he did not enter Man o' War in the Kentucky Derby, preferring to start with the Preakness at a mile and one eighth later in the month.

After Man o' War was his, Riddle had him broken at Saratoga before shipping him to his Glen Riddle Farm on Maryland's Eastern Shore. Before many months had passed, Riddle knew that his first impressions of Man o' War had been right. In the early spring of 1919 Riddle shipped him to Belmont Park to get ready for the juvenile classics. The colt's speedy workouts were soon the talk of the backstretch.

Unlike most fast-moving thoroughbreds, which run economically close to the ground, their hoofs shaving the turf, as it were, Big Red rolled along with tremendous jack-rabbitlike bounds, his stride measuring nearly ten yards. From a distance he appeared to be floating in slow motion. Only when spectators turned their field glasses on the horses running in the dust behind him was it possible for them to get a true sense of the blinding pace he was setting.

Feustel picked the sixth race on June 6, 1919, for Man o' War's debut, a five-furlong test for maiden two-year-olds over a straight course. In the paddock, beneath the wide-spreading chestnuts and oaks, the immemorial pageant repeated itself, owners and trainers leaning down to give last-minute instructions to cocky little men in shimmering silks. With his straw boater, bristling mustache, and florid complexion, Samuel D. Riddle looked every inch the expectant owner; Feustel fitted the role of the confident young trainer; and Johnny Loftus, in Riddle's black and yellow silks, was very much the bantam rooster.

As the bugler blew "First Call," Feustel told Loftus not to break the colt at the barrier: "Wait until they get out of your way, Johnny, then let him go after them."

At the start, Loftus let his six opponents break ahead and then gave chase. Before a hundred yards had been covered, Man o' War was up with the leaders. At the first furlong pole Loftus gave him free rein, and in a few strides the race was all but over. Man o' War dashed out in front; Loftus, looking for possible contenders and fearing someone might be sneaking up on the rail, turned to his left and to his right. With no horse close by, he began to pull up and was standing straight up in the stirrups at the finish line. Man o' War had raced the five eighths of a mile in fifty-nine seconds, finishing five lengths ahead of his closest rival. As the *Morning Telegraph* reported next day, Big Red "made a half-a-dozen high-class youngsters look like $200 horses."

With his first race, Big Red set a pattern that he was to follow, almost without exception, throughout the remaining twenty races of his career. In the two years that he ran, he won twenty of his twenty-one races. His margins of victory ranged from a single length in two victories as a two-year-old to one hundred lengths when he won the Lawrence Realization at Belmont Park in September of 1920, defeating the only other horse in the race, an animal named Hoodwink.

Although today's two-year-olds rarely carry more than 122 pounds, Man o' War was handicapped at 130 pounds on six occasions. When three, in the Potomac Handicap at Havre de Grace, Maryland, he carried 138 pounds on a heavy, cuppy track and whipped the ears off a field of thoroughbreds.

As a three-year-old, Man o' War set North American records for the mile (1:35 4/5); mile and one eighth (1:49 1/5); mile and three eighths (2:14 1/5); mile and one half (2:28 4/5); and mile and five eighths (2:40 4/5). All but the record for the mile and three eighths have since been eclipsed, which was to be expected. For one thing, racing surfaces today are considered a good two seconds faster per mile than they were in his day; for another, thoroughbreds now wear aluminum shoes, faster by far than the steel shoes worn by Man o' War and his contemporaries. The lone record survives because a mile-and-three-eighths race is now infrequently run on a dirt (as opposed to grass) track.

To this day, an air of mystery surrounds Man o' War's only loss, in the Sanford Memorial at Saratoga on August 13, 1919. By that time Big Red boasted a string of six easy victories, all under jockey Johnny Loftus.

The morning of the race, Willie Knapp, who was to ride a colt named Upset from the Harry Payne Whitney stable, was sitting with Jim Rowe, Whitney's trainer, on the steps of Rowe's cottage. "You know, Mr. Rowe, we got a chance to beat Man o' War this afternoon," said Knapp.

As Man o' War had beaten Upset soundly in their last race, Rowe replied, "Willie, you're the craziest man I ever heard of."

Man o' War was in at 130 pounds, along with Golden Broom, owned by Mrs. Walter M. Jeffords, Mrs. Riddle's niece. Upset was to carry 115 pounds. Donnacona, The Swimmer, Armistice, and Captain Alcock completed the field for the six-furlong sprint.

Saratoga's regular starter was ill on the day of the Sanford, and his place was taken by C. H. Pettingill, an aging racing official. Nearly thirty years earlier Pettingill had attained a measure of fame by allowing a field of horses at Washington Park in Chicago to mill around for an hour and a half before he sprang the tape.

Down below the starter's stand the graceful two-year-olds whirled, their jockeys maneuvering for place, crowding one another, eyes cocked on old Pettingill. Each time Man o' War lunged, Knapp kept Upset right with him; then the pair turned around and tried to get lined up again. On the fifth lunge, Knapp yelled: "Johnny, let's back up this time and maybe we can get a start."

Loftus started to back up his mount and Knapp followed suit, but just for a step or two. Then he braced himself, ready to go. At that instant the tape flew up, the jockeys let out a whoop, and Golden Broom was off winging, his four white-stockinged legs driving like pistons. Upset was on his quarters, followed by Armistice and Donnacona. The jockeys aboard The Swimmer and Captain Alcock had been caught off guard and were now scrambling to get under way. Together with Man o' War, also caught flat-footed, they were left at the post.

Big Red leapt forward and pounded down the track, nearly running into The Swimmer and Captain Alcock when they swerved across in front of him, causing Loftus to yank on the reins and lose more precious seconds. Loftus drove to the outside, trying to get past the horses between him and the front runners. Golden Broom was cutting a hole in the wind, with Upset still up close, moving easily. Flying into the turn for home, Golden Broom was on the rail, Upset on the outside, with Man o' War now in third position.

There was no way for Man o' War to get through unless Loftus took him to the outside again. Instead, he tried to fight his way between the two horses.

"We'd passed the quarter pole and were going to the eighth pole when I heard something right behind me and I knew it was Big Red coming at me now," says Knapp. "I looked back and there he was. Johnny Loftus was riding like a crazy man and he yelled at me: 'Move over, Willie! I'm coming through!' So I yelled at him: 'Take off! Take off, you bum, or I'll put you through the rail!' "

Loftus swerved to the outside, and at that moment, with less than a sixteenth of a mile to go, Knapp went to the whip and Upset surged ahead of a sagging Golden Broom. Man o' War and Upset ran for the wire, Big Red gaining with every stride, passing Upset with a giant bound—but a split second after they had crossed the finish line. It was Upset by a half length.

Loftus came back to win three more big races on Man o' War—the Grand Union Hotel Stakes and the Hopeful Stakes at Saratoga, and the Futurity at Belmont Park—to wind up the horse's two-year-old year. In all three races Big Red left Upset in the ruck, and in the Futurity he also beat Upset's stablemates, Dr. Clark and John P. Grier.

William H. P. Robertson, editor of the *Thoroughbred Record* and author of *The History of Thoroughbred Racing in America*, believes that too much has been made of the Sanford and that it would long since have been forgotten

Always playful, Man o' War was a frisky twenty-two when photographed below, and still rearing up at twenty-seven (right). On his thirtieth, and last, birthday in 1947 (opposite page), he sniffed appreciatively at a floral wreath sent by an admirer.

WIDE WORLD

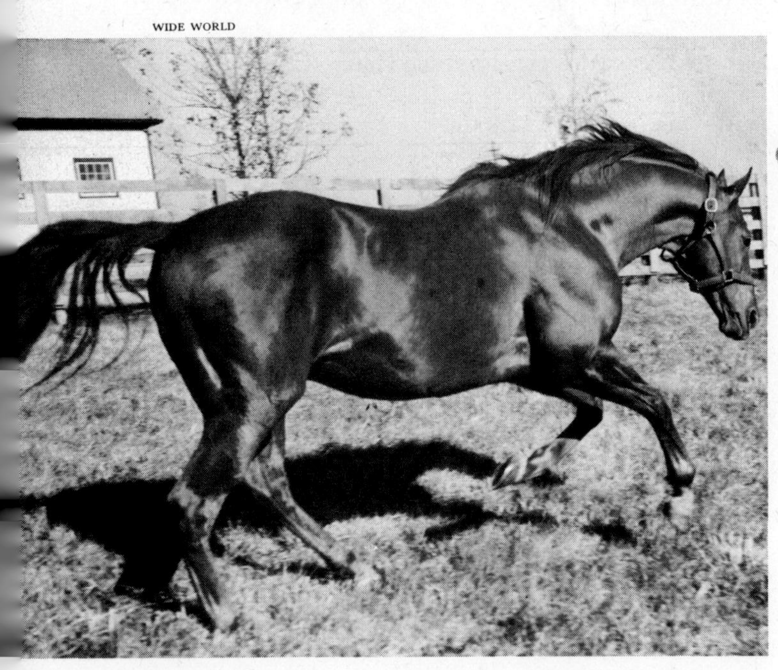

UPI

had Big Red not gone on to such glory. In Robertson's view, Man o' War in 1919 was just another high-flying two-year-old that had its wings clipped after a poor ride and bad racing luck.

After the Futurity at Belmont, Man o' War was unwound for a week and then shipped back to Glen Riddle Farm to enjoy a winter free of racing. At the same time, Jim Rowe began laying plans to humble him once again.

Rowe was one of the fine trainers of his day, but he was not a graceful loser. He was incensed when sportswriters considered Upset's victory in the Sanford a fluke or worse, and he was not pleased when Man o' War whipped Upset every time they met thereafter. Rowe was somewhat spoiled, for each year Whitney's Brookdale Stud produced at least half a dozen classy youngsters for him to campaign in the big juvenile races. He was in the habit of winning these races, and Big Red had put a stop to it. With Wildair, John P. Grier, Upset, Damask, and Dr. Clark, Rowe raced against Man o' War seventeen times and won only once, with Upset in the Sanford. John P. Grier, however, threw a real scare into the wonder horse in what was certainly one of the most exciting horse races in American history.

Although the 1920 season was again proving a winning one for Man o' War, the strain of campaigning a public idol began to show in Feustel and Riddle, and relations between the two men went from bad to worse. Feustel was a temperamental individual and he took justifiable pride in his handling of Man o' War.

Big Red was served his first meal at 3:30 A.M. Then he lolled in his stall until 7:30, when Frank Loftus curried and brushed him, combed his mane and tail, bathed his feet and head, and sponged out his eyes and nostrils.

At 8:30 Man o' War was exercised. He jogged half a mile and galloped a mile and a half three days a week. Every Tuesday, Thursday, and Saturday he was given fast workouts on the track. After that, he was walked until he had cooled off and then was bathed with a mixture of alcohol, arnica, and witch hazel to keep his muscles from getting stiff. Afterward, the bandages that he always wore except when racing were changed, and his hoofs were washed again.

Man o' War had lunch at 11:30. He took a final half-hour walk at 4, and at 5:15 his final meal of the day. He ordinarily ate twelve quarts of oats (twelve and a half on racing days)—or three quarts a day more than the average racehorse consumes when in training.

Of an evening Feustel, his stable foreman, George Conway, and the inevitable hangers-on would set up a table in front of Big Red's stall and play cards. When they departed, Frank Loftus or Conway or some stable-hand slept on a cot in an adjoining stall, for warnings were forever reaching Riddle that "something is going to happen" to Man o' War, and "look out for it." As it turned out, these rumors were not without foundation.

But for all the care that Feustel lavished on Man o'

WIDE WORLD

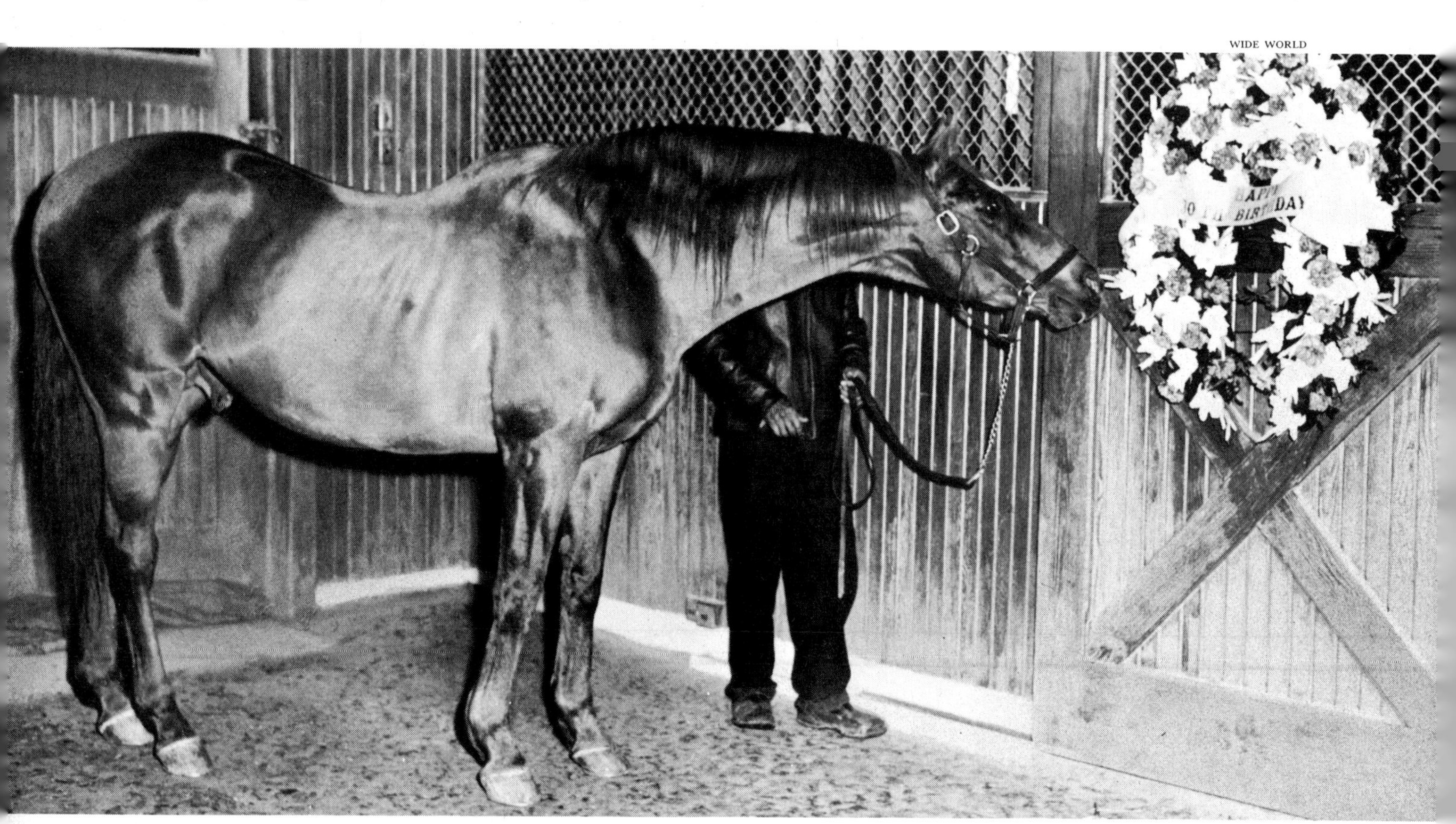

War, Riddle apparently wasn't satisfied. He hired a private detective to watch Feustel.

Toward the end of Man o' War's three-year-old year, few owners were willing to send their horses out to eat his dust. On four occasions only one other horse could be found to face him at the post; on three occasions he went off at odds of 1 to 100 (even so, one professional gambler reportedly bet $100,000 on him for a return of $1,000). The charts of Man o' War's races in the *Daily Racing Form* of fifty years ago invariably read: "won easily," "won cantering," or "won eased up." Nevertheless, Feustel's archrival, Jim Rowe, was determined to defeat the champion again, this time with John P. Grier.

The crowd at Aqueduct Racetrack, Long Island, on July 10, 1920, numbered 25,000, the largest then in its history. They had come to see the Dwyer Stakes, in which only two horses were entered: John P. Grier and Man o' War. The race was at a mile and one eighth, and Rowe had been carefully honing Grier for the test. At a mile, there were few faster horses in the country.

The Dwyer was, in effect, a match race. Before the race, Rowe went out on a long limb. "We'll see if Man o' War can beat a horse that can stay with him all the way," he told reporters. "I think he's ready to be taken, and Grier is the horse that can do it." One tactless newspaperman noted that Man o' War had had little trouble beating John P. Grier as a two-year-old. "That was *last* year," said Rowe. "This is a different year, and an improved horse."

Man o' War had been campaigning hard and steadily, following up the Preakness with victories in the Withers and Belmont Stakes at Belmont Park and the Stuyvesant at Jamaica. Some people wondered whether Big Red might not have lost his edge. In addition, Grier was in at 108 pounds against 126 for Man o' War. Eddie Ambrose, one of the nation's hottest jockeys, would wear Whitney's blue silks and brown cap.

All of this produced an unsettling atmosphere in the Riddle barn. Big Red's handlers developed a case of the whammies. "Man o' War isn't screwed up as tight as he might be," Feustel told Riddle. And in the paddock before the race, Riddle cautioned jockey Clarence Kummer: "Lay along with Grier all the way, and if you find you can win, don't try to ride him out, but win by a length or two. I don't want more made of Red than is necessary."

At the starting post in the back shoot, Man o' War was on the rail, compact little Grier on the outside. A great roar came from the crowd as the race got under way. Many in the grandstand thought at first that Grier had been left at the post, for they could not see him, running, as he was, stride for stride on the far side of Big Red.

The two horses hit the half-mile mark in 46 seconds flat, a track record; the five-furlong marker in 57 2/5 seconds, a track record; the three-quarter pole in 1:09 3/5, a track record; the mile in 1:36 flat, a track record. No horse had ever been able to stay with Man o' War in this fashion, and it became obvious that one of them had to crack, and crack soon.

Kummer went to the whip, and Man o' War regained the lead by a hair. Down to the wire they came, and then it happened: seventy yards short of the finish, Grier

A bugler wearing the Riddle Farm's black and yellow silks played taps at Man o' War's funeral services in Lexington, Kentucky, in 1947. Nearly two thousand horse lovers attended the ceremony, which was broadcast by radio nationwide and described by one newspaper reporter as "probably the most elaborate last rites ever for an animal."

wilted. Ambrose smacked him once more with the whip, but when the little colt failed to respond, he eased up.

The Dwyer was the high-water mark of Man o' War's career. Never again would he be tested in this manner. Steam poured off his trembling body as he was walked back to the stables and sloshed with water. After Big Red had dried out, Frank Loftus tossed a black and yellow cooler blanket over him and walked him around the shed row for half an hour, occasionally feeding him a piece of sugar. Then he turned the horse loose in his stall of fresh, sweet-smelling rye straw. Man o' War lay right down and slept for hours.

The last race of Man o' War's career was an unfortunate anticlimax, marked by evidence of attempted foul play. This was the match race at Kenilworth Park, Windsor, Ontario, on October 12, 1920, against Sir Barton, the four-year-old champion, at a mile and one quarter for a purse of $75,000 and a $5,000 gold cup.

In 1919, when Man o' War had been cleaning up the two-year-old classics, Sir Barton had become the first horse to win the Kentucky Derby, Preakness, and Belmont Stakes. He was a magnificent animal, and it should have been a great race. But as so often happens in carefully arranged match races, one horse or the other fails to come up to the race in top form. Sir Barton wasn't himself that day, and the track, dry and brick-hard, was not to his liking. Moreover, at the last minute his owner, J. K. L. Ross, of Canada, announced that his regular rider, Earl Sande, was being replaced "without prejudice" by jockey Frank Keough. No reason was given, but it was common knowledge that Ross had never forgiven Sande for saying, after his one ride aboard Man o' War, that Big Red was the greatest horse he had ever ridden.

Man o' War, the betting favorite, breezed home in easy fashion. But just as Big Red passed the finish line, Kummer stood up in his irons and his right stirrup leather broke, nearly causing him to fall. Had the leather given way seconds before, he might have been seriously injured or even killed. Back in the paddock, Feustel and Kummer examined the stirrup leather carefully. It had been partly severed by a sharp instrument. Who did it or why was never discovered.

Afterward, when the Jockey Club handicapper indicated that Man o' War would have to carry even greater weights if he ran as a four-year-old, Riddle decided to retire the champion to stud. On the way south to his stud farm in Kentucky, Riddle displayed his horse to friends at the Rose Tree Hunt, outside Philadelphia. A great crowd showed up to pay tribute to the horse, Jack Dempsey and Bill Tilden among those who had journeyed to see him for the last time. And at the old Kentucky Association track in Lexington, Man o' War was cantered around for yet another tribute.

Big Red had already given birth to the star system, which has had so much to do with transforming horse racing and breeding from a sport enjoyed by a handful of Whitneys, Wideners, Vanderbilts, and Phippses to the huge industry it is today, wherein a Buckpasser, say, can win more than $1,400,000 on the turf and then be syndicated at stud for nearly $5,000,000. Thoroughbred racing now boasts a yearly attendance of more than 40,000,000 persons at one hundred racetracks in twenty-eight states offering sixty races valued at $100,000 and up. Man o' War's earnings total of $249,465 would be considered peanuts today, but it was enough to make him the all-time money winner as of 1920.

During the more than twenty years that Man o' War was at stud, hundreds of thousands of visitors filed through Riddle's Faraway Farm to see the legendary chestnut and hear groom Will Harbut's spiel: "He was folded March 29, 1917, at Major Belmont's place, right over there. Mr. Riddle bought him for $5,000 at Saratoga as a yearling. . . . A man come here and offered a million dollars for him, and Mr. Riddles said no, lots of men might have a million dollars, but only one man could have Man o' War. . . ."

"Yes, sir, we turns him out every day. . . ."

"No, ma'am, he ain't no trotter. . . ."

"Stand still, Red!"

Man o' War died of a heart attack at 12:15 P.M. on November 1, 1947, at the age of thirty. He had sired 386 registered foals, more than half of whom were winners, though none ever matched its father's accomplishments. His funeral attracted a large crowd and in a tribute to Big Red at his death, *The Blood-Horse* magazine said:

> Some others will remember the day he came back home to Kentucky and, under colors for the last time, was cantered along the sloppy stretch of the old Kentucky Association track, the faint light of winter gleaming on his golden coat.
>
> The horsemen who came from all over the world to see him in his prime at Faraway will remember him vividly—the massive body, the wide sweeps of muscle, the great chest and abnormally wide spacing between his fore legs, the die-cut perfection of his legs and feet, the slight dip of the back deepening with the years, the high head, the imperial air, the feel of power and mastery. They will not look to see another like him.

But the tribute that has lasted for all the years since Man o' War's death was uttered by Will Harbut, who died just twenty-nine days before the champion: "He was de mostest hoss."

A staff writer for the National Observer *and a previous contributor to this magazine, Mr. Chew has been interested in the equine species since he exercised hunters and steeplechasers as a boy in Virginia. He was the recipient of the Magazine Journalism Award of the Thoroughbred Racing Association in 1969 for his article on trainer John Cotter and his wife, Mary, a show rider.*

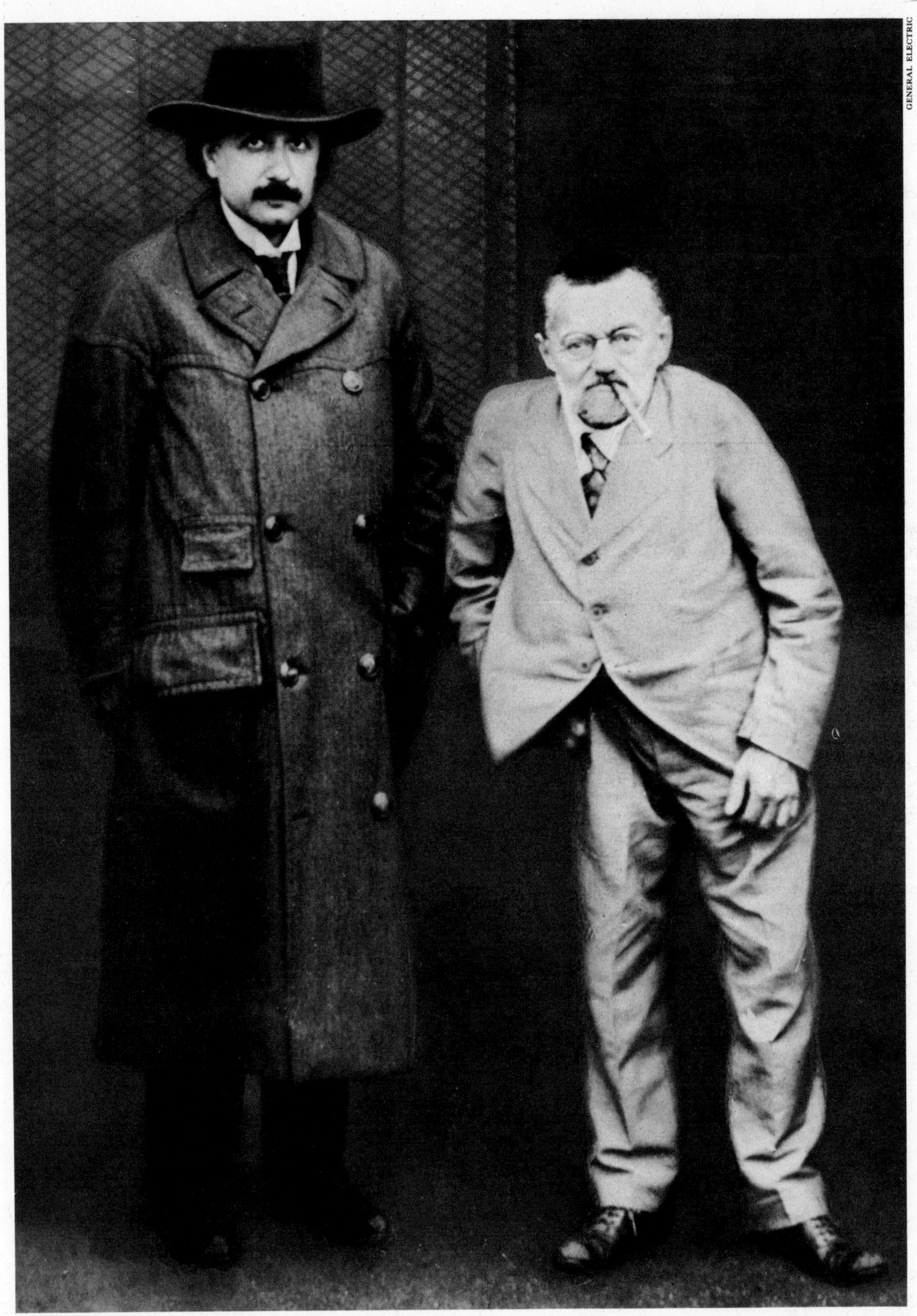

GENERAL ELECTRIC

Garbed in full Middle European fashion, Albert Einstein, who was soon to be awarded the Nobel Prize in physics, visited Charles P. Steinmetz in Schenectady in 1921. The latter then worked for General Electric and taught at Union College.

Dos Passos: The Wizards Meet

Steinmetz was a hunchback,
son of a hunchback lithographer.

He was born in Breslau in eighteen sixtyfive, graduated with highest honors at seventeen from the Breslau Gymnasium, went to the University of Breslau to study mathematics;

mathematics to Steinmetz was muscular strength and long walks over the hills and the kiss of a girl in love and big evenings spent swilling beer with your friends;

on his broken back he felt the topheavy weight of society the way workingmen felt it on their straight backs, the way poor students felt it, was a member of a socialist club, editor of a paper called *The People's Voice*.

Bismarck was sitting in Berlin like a big paperweight to keep the new Germany feudal, to hold down the empire for his bosses the Hohenzollerns.

Steinmetz had to run off to Zurich for fear of going to jail; at Zurich his mathematics woke up all the professors at the Polytechnic;

but Europe in the eighties was no place for a penniless German student with a broken back and a big head filled with symbolic calculus and wonder about electricity that is mathematics made power

and a socialist at that.

With a Danish friend he sailed for America steerage on an old French line boat *La Champagne*,

lived in Brooklyn at first and commuted to Yonkers where he had a twelvedollar a week job with Rudolph Eichemeyer who was a German exile from fortyeight an inventor and electrician and owner of a factory where he made hatmaking machinery and electrical generators.

In Yonkers he worked out the theory of the Third Harmonics

and the law of hysteresis which states in a formula the hundredfold relations between the metallic heat, density, frequency when the poles change places in the core of a magnet under an alternating current.

It is Steinmetz's law of hysteresis that makes possible all the transformers that crouch in little boxes and gable-roofed houses in all the hightension lines all over everywhere. The mathematical symbols of Steinmetz's law are the patterns of all transformers everywhere.

In eighteen ninetytwo when Eichemeyer sold out to the corporation that was to form General Electric, Steinmetz was entered in the contract along with other valuable apparatus. All his life Steinmetz was a piece of apparatus belonging to General Electric.

First his laboratory was at Lynn, then it was moved and the little hunchback with it to Schenectady, the electric city.

General Electric humored him, let him be a socialist, let him keep a greenhouseful of cactuses lit up by mercury lights, let him have alligators, talking crows and a gila monster for pets and the publicity department talked up the wizard, the medicine man who knew the symbols that opened up the doors of Ali Baba's cave.

Steinmetz jotted a formula on his cuff and next morning a thousand new powerplants had sprung up and the dynamos sang dollars and the silence of the transformers was all dollars,

and the publicity department poured oily stories into the ears of the American public every Sunday and Steinmetz became the little parlor magician,

who made a toy thunderstorm in his laboratory and made all the toy trains run on time and the meat stay cold in the icebox and the lamp in the parlor and the great lighthouses and the searchlights and the revolving beams of light that guide airplanes at night towards Chicago, New York, St. Louis, Los Angeles,

and they let him be a socialist and believe that human society could be improved the way you can improve a dynamo and they let him be pro-German and write a letter offering his services to Lenin because mathematicians are so impractical who make up formulas by which you can build powerplants, factories, subway systems, light, heat, air, sunshine but not human relations that affect the stockholders' money and the directors' salaries.

Steinmetz was a famous magician and he talked to Edison tapping with the Morse code on Edison's knee

because Edison was so very deaf
and he went out West
to make speeches that nobody understood
and he talked to Bryan about God on a railroad train
and all the reporters stood round while he and Einstein
met face to face,
but they couldn't catch what they said
and Steinmetz was the most valuable piece of apparatus General Electric had
until he wore out and died.

John Dos Passos died last September, much to the sorrow of this magazine, to which he had contributed frequently in recent years. He had turned from the novel to formal history, but in his youth he had already shown a great flair for bringing the past to life in idiosyncratic "prose poems," of which the above is a fine sample. It comes from his 1930 novel, The 42nd Parallel, *but seems rather appropriate to a time when science and technology are overwhelming us. Our thanks for the opportunity to reprint it go to the Houghton Mifflin Company, which now has in its hands a new novel that Dos Passos completed shortly before his death.* —The Editors

Voices of Lexington and Concord

CONTINUED FROM PAGE 13

words of Colonel Francis Smith, the expedition's top commander:

Our troops advanced toward them, without any intention of injuring them, further than to inquire the reason of their being thus assembled, and if not satisfactory, to have secured their arms; but they in confusion went off, principally to the left—only one of them fired before he went off, and three or four more jumped over a wall and fired from behind it among the soldiers; on which the troops returned it. . . .

It was never to be ascertained who fired the first shot. The Americans, who were hopelessly outnumbered, shortly began dispersing. But at least some of the men stood their ground long enough to take some British fire. One of these was Lieutenant William Tidd:

They . . . fired upon us. I then retreated up the north road, and was pursued about thirty rods by an officer on horseback (supposed to be Maj. Pitcairn), calling out to me, "Damn you, stop, or you are a dead man!" I found I could not escape him unless I left the road. Therefore I sprang over a pair of bars, made a stand, and discharged my gun at him; upon which he immediately returned to the main body. . . .

Corporal John Munroe's departure from the field was less precipitate:

After the first fire of the regulars, I thought, and so stated to Ebenezer Munroe . . . who stood next to me on the left, that they had fired nothing but powder; but, on the second firing, Munroe said they had fired something more than powder, for he had received a wound in his arm; and now, said he, to use his own words, "I'll give them the guts of my gun." We then both took aim at the main body of the British troops—the smoke preventing our seeing anything but the heads of some of their horses—and discharged our pieces.

After the second fire from the British troops, I distinctly saw Jonas Parker struggling on the ground, with his gun in his hand, apparently attempting to load it. In this situation the British came up, run him through with the bayonet, and killed him on the spot.

After I had fired the first time, I retreated about ten rods, and then loaded my gun a second time, with two balls, and, on firing at the British, the strength of the charge took off about a foot of my gun barrel. Such was the general confusion, and so much firing on the part of the British, that it was impossible for me to know the number of our men who fired immediately on receiving the second fire from the British troops; but that some of them fired, besides Ebenezer Munroe and myself, I am very confident.

The regulars kept up a fire, in all directions, as long as they could see a man of our company in arms. Isaac Muzzy, Jonathan Harrington, and my father, Robert Munroe [died] near the place where our line was formed. Samuel Hadley and John Brown were killed after they had gotten off the common. Asahel Porter, of Woburn, who had been taken a prisoner by the British on their march to Lexington, attempted to make his escape, and was shot within a few rods of the common. Caleb Harrington was shot down on attempting to leave the meeting-house, where he and some others had gone, before the British soldiers came up, for the purpose of removing a quantity of powder that was stored there.

Elijah Sanderson was a witness to one of the fight's closing incidents:

After our militia had dispersed, I saw [the British] firing at one man (Solomon Brown), who was stationed behind a wall. I saw the wall smoke with the bullets hitting it. . . . [Brown] fired into a solid column of them, and then retreated. He was in the cow yard. The wall saved him. He legged it just about the time I went away.

Eight Americans were killed and about ten were wounded in the brief encounter. When it was over, the British fired a victory volley into the air and gave three cheers. Soon afterward, to the tune of fife and drum, they headed for Concord. According to Ebenezer Munroe:

After they had marched off . . . we took two prisoners who were considerably in the rear of the main body. I carried their arms into Buckman's tavern, and they were taken by some of our men who had none of their own. I believed, at the time, that some of our shots must have [taken effect]. I was afterwards confirmed in this opinion. . . .

A Lexington boy named Abijah Harrington, who had two brothers in the fight but was too young to take part, was to remember through the years:

I went up to the meeting-house soon after the regulars had marched off for Concord, and, at the distance of about ten or twelve rods below the meeting-house, where I was told the main body of their troops stood when they were fired upon by our militia, I distinctly saw blood on the ground, in the road, and, the ground being a little descending, the blood had run along the road about six or eight feet.

Actually, the British had suffered only two casualties. One man had been hit in the leg, and one in the hand. In addition, Major Pitcairn reported that his horse had been wounded in two places by shots that came "from one quarter or another." According to Lieutenant Barker, of the King's Own, the British march to Concord was uneventful:

We met with no interruption till within a mile or two of the town, where the country people had occupied a hill which commanded the road.

One of the "country people" was Concord Minuteman Thaddeus Blood:

We . . . saw the British troops acoming. . . . The sun was rising and shined on their arms, and they made a noble appearance in their red coats and glistening arms.

Lieutenant Barker continues:

The Light Infantry were ordered away to the right and ascended the height in one line, upon which the Yankies quitted it without firing, which they did likewise for one or two more successively. . . . [We took] possession of a hill with a Liberty Pole on it and a flag flying, which was cut down. The Yankies had that hill, but left it to us. We expected they would have made a stand there, but they did not chuse it.

In the words of Minuteman Amos Barrett:

We . . . marched before them with our drums and fifes a-going, and also the British. We had grand musick. . . . We marched into town and over the north bridge a little more than half a mile, and then on a hill . . . where we could see and hear what was going on. . . .

One of the village residents who watched the scarlet columns approach was Martha Moulton. A poor "widow woman," she was later to petition the province for a financial reward (which she was granted) for her part in the day's activities:

. . . [They], in a hostile manner, entered the town and drawed up in form before the door of the house where I live; and there they continued on the green, feeding their horses within five feet of the door; and about fifty or sixty of them was in and out the house, calling for water and what they wanted. . . . At the same time, all our near neighbors, in the greatest consternation, were drawn off to places far from the thickest part of the town, where I live, and had taken with them their families and what of their best effects they could carry—some to a neighboring wood, and others to remote houses. . . .

Your petitioner, being left to the mercy of six or seven hundred armed men, and no person near but an old man of eighty-five years, and myself seventy-one years old, and both very infirm. It may be easily imagined what a sad condition your petitioner must be in. Under these circumstances, your petitioner committed herself, more especially, to the Divine Protection, and was very remarkably helpt with so much fortitude of mind, as to wait on them, as they called for water, or what we had—chairs for Major Pitcairn and four or five more officers—who sat at the door viewing their men. At length your petitioner had, by degrees, cultivated so much favor as to talk a little with them.

At this point it must be noted that not all of the British troops remained near Martha Moulton's house. The movements of one detachment are explained by a British ensign named Henry D'Bernicre, who was acquainted with Concord, having been there a few weeks earlier as a spy:

Capt. Parsons of the 10th was dispatched with six light companies to take possession of a bridge that lay three-quarters of a mile [north of] Concord, and I was ordered to shew him the road there, and also to conduct him to a house where there was some cannon and other stores hid. When we arrived at the bridge, three companies under the command of Capt. [Lawrie] of the 43d were left to protect it. These three companies were not close together, but situated so as to be able to support each other. We then proceeded to Col. Barrett's, where the stores were. We did not find so much as we expected, but what there was we destroyed.

There was an excellent reason why few important stores were found at Barrett's—or elsewhere. The Patriots had been alerted early enough so that, working urgently, they were able to transfer some of the things to safer towns and to hide other items in cellars, attics, and nearby patches of woods. At the North Bridge the situation was now becoming taut. The Americans who had occupied the hill—men of Concord and neighboring Lincoln—were being joined by militia units from other villages scattered about Concord; and as the force increased in size it increased also in aggressive spirit. Among the British officers who anticipated trouble was Lieutenant Barker:

During this time the people were gathering together in great numbers, and, taking advantage of our scattered disposition, seemed as if they were going to cut off the communication with the bridge, upon which the two [farther] companies joined and went to the bridge to support that company. The three companies drew up in the road the far side the bridge, and the rebels on the hill above, covered by a wall. In that situation they remained a long time, very near an hour, the three companies expecting to be attacked by the rebels. . . .

Captn. Lawrie, who commanded these three companies, sent to Col. Smith begging he would send more troops to his assistance and informing him of his situation. The Col. ordered 2 or 3 companies, but put himself at their head, by which means stopt 'em from being time enough, for being a very fat heavy man he would not have reached the bridge in half an hour, though it was not half a mile to it.

In Concord, Martha Moulton was still having her troubles:

When all on a sudden they had set fire to the great gun carriages just by the house, and while they were in flames, your petitioner saw smoke arise out of the Town House higher than the ridge of the house. Then your petitioner did put her life, as it were, in her hand, and ventured to beg of the officers to send some of their men to put out the fire; but they took no notice, only sneered. Your petitioner, seeing the Town House on fire, and must in a few munutes be past recovery, did yet venture to expostulate with the officers just by her, as she stood with a pail of water in her hand, begging of them to send, etc. When they only said, "O, mother, we won't do you any harm!" "Don't be concerned, mother!" and such like talk.

The house still burning, and knowing that all the row of four or five houses, as well as the school house, was in certain danger, your petitioner (not knowing but she might provoke them by her insufficient pleading) yet ventured to put as much strength to her arguments as an unfortunate widow could think of; and so your petitioner can safely say that, under Divine Providence, she was an instrument of saving the Court House, and how many more is not certain, from being consumed, with a great deal of valuable furniture, and at the great risk of her life. At last, by one pail of water after another, they sent and did extinguish the fire.

Seeing the smoke rising from the village angered the Americans at the bridge. Those who lived in Concord decided that it was time they made a move to defend their homes. At this point a militia company from Acton, commanded by Captain Isaac Davis, joined the murmuring troops. Among the newcomers was Thomas Thorp:

We found a great collection of armed men, from Concord and other towns; there were several hundreds, cannot say how many. The officers seemed to be talking by themselves, and the British were then at the bridge. Our officers joined the others; and in a few minutes, not exceeding five, Captain Davis returned to his company and drew his sword, and said to the company, "I haven't a man that is afraid to go," and gave the word "March!"

With fifers and drummers playing an especially lively tune called "The White Cockade," the aggregation headed down the hill toward the bridge. There was a general determination "to march into the middle of the town for its defence, or die in the attempt." Major John Buttrick, of Concord, was in charge. The leading unit was the thirty-eight-man Acton company under Isaac Davis.

Lieutenant Barker, of the King's Own, describes the British reaction:

The rebels marched into the road and were coming down upon us, when Captain Lawrie made his men retire to this side the bridge (which bye the bye he ought to have done at first), and then he would have had time to make a good disposition, but at this time he had not, for the rebels were got so near him that his people were obliged to form the best way they could. As soon as they were got over the bridge the three companies got one behind the other so that only the front one could fire.

A few of the redcoats had been ordered to linger on the bridge and try to make it impassable by removing some of the planks. This caused Major Buttrick to protest loudly, and he and the other leading Americans quickened their step. The British effort, begun too late anyway, was abandoned. According to Lieutenant Barker:

The fire soon began from a dropping shot on our side. . . .

Minuteman Thaddeus Blood confirms this:

I saw where the ball threw up the water about the middle of the river, and then a second and third shot [did the same]. . . .

These were intended as warning shots. But the Americans didn't stop. Now the British fired for effect; and Major Buttrick, hearing a young Acton fifer cry out that he had been hit, shouted, "Fire. . . . For God's sake, fire!" In a general exchange that lasted but a few minutes, two Americans and two redcoats were killed. The Americans had only two or three wounded, while the British had about ten. One of the Americans slain was the gallant Captain Davis. His widow was later to write:

He was then thirty years of age. We had four children; the youngest about fifteen months old. They were all unwell when he left me in the morning; some of them with the canker-rash. . . . My husband said little that morning. He seemed serious and thoughtful; but never seemed to hesitate as to the course of his duty. As he led the company from the house, he turned himself round, and seemed to have something to communicate. He only said, "Take good care of the children," and was soon out of sight.

Observing the skirmish through a window of a nearby house (the Manse) was the Reverend William Emerson, grandfather of the more famous Emerson. He says of the British:

The three companies . . . soon quitted their post at the bridge and retreated in the greatest disorder and confusion to the main body, who were soon upon the march to meet them.

As the redcoats retreated, the Americans swept across the bridge. But, according to Amos Barrett, they went no farther:

We did not follow them. There was 8 or 10 that was wounded and a running and a hobbling about, looking back to see if we was after them. We then saw the whole body a coming out of town. We were ordered to lay behind a wall that run over a hill, and when they got nigh enough, Major Buttrick said he would give the word fire. But they did not come quite so near as he expected, before they halted. The commanding officer ordered the whole battalion to halt, and officers to the front; the officers then marched to the front; then we lay behind the wall, about 200 of us, with our guns cocked, expecting every minute to have the word fire. Our orders was if we fired, to fire 2 or three times and then retreat. If we had fired, I believe we could have killed almost every officer there was in the front; but we had no orders to fire. . . . They staid about 10 minutes and then marched back. . . .

The Reverend Mr. Emerson writes:

For half an hour, the enemy, by their marches and countermarches, discovered great fickleness and inconstancy of mind, sometimes advancing, sometimes returning to their former posts; till at length they quitted the town and retreated by the way they came.

In the meantime, a party of our men (150) took the back way through the Great Fields into the east quarter and had placed themselves to advantage, lying in ambush behind walls, fences and buildings, ready to fire upon the enemy on their retreat.

These men were joined by other troops newly arrived in the Concord area. Says Edmund Foster, of Reading:

A little before we came to Merriam's Hill, we discovered the enemy's flank guard, of about eighty or one hundred men, who, on their retreat from Concord, kept that height of land, the main body in the road. The British troops and the Americans, at that time, were equally distant from Merriam's Corner. About twenty rods short of that place, the Americans made a halt.

The British marched down the hill, with very slow but steady step, without music, or a word being spoken that could be heard. Silence reigned on both sides.

As soon as the British had gained the main road, and passed a small bridge near that corner, they faced about suddenly, and fired a volley of musketry upon us. They overshot; and no one, to my knowledge, was injured by the fire. The fire was immediately returned by the Americans, and two British soldiers fell dead, at a little distance from each other, in the road, near the brook.

The British continued to retreat, and the Americans pursued. Foster goes on:

We saw a wood at a distance which appeared to lie on or near the road where the enemy must pass. Many leaped over the walls and made for that wood. We arrived just in time to meet the enemy. There was on the opposite side of the road a young growth of wood, filled with Americans. The enemy were now completely between two fires, renewed and briskly kept up. They ordered out a flank guard on the left to dislodge the Americans from their posts behind the trees; but they only became better marks to be shot at.

Ensign D'Bernicre describes the distress of the British:

All the hills on each side of us were covered with rebels . . . so that they kept the road always lined and a very hot fire on us without intermission. We at first kept our order, and returned their fire as hot as we received it; but when we arrived within a mile of Lexington, our ammunition began to fail, and the light companies were so fatigued with flanking they were scarce able to act; and a great number of wounded scarce able to get forward made a great confusion.

The unfortunate redcoats must have felt mortification as well as fear during these moments. Just a few hours before, they had been Lexington's masters. In the best romantic tradition the anguished men received help from Boston at the instant of their greatest need. First they heard the distant sound of martial music. Then Brigadier General Earl Percy, astride a beautiful white horse, swung into sight leading about a thousand reinforcements. The troops had come in answer to a request Colonel Smith had sent back to Boston early in the morning. D'Bernicre exults:

[Percy] brought two field-pieces with him, which were immediately brought to bear upon the rebels, and soon silenced their fire. After a little firing [our whole body] halted for about half an hour to rest.

Lord Percy tells how the British march was resumed:

As it began now to grow pretty late, and we had 15 miles to retire, and only our 36 rounds [each], I ordered the Grenadiers and Light Infantry to move off first, and covered them with my Brigade, sending out very strong flanking parties, which were absolutely necessary. . . .

D'Bernicre adds:

The rebels . . . kept firing on us, but very lightly until we came to Menotomy [Arlington], a village with a number of houses in little groups extending about half a mile. Out of these houses they kept a very heavy fire. . . . The soldiers shewed great bravery in this place, forcing houses . . . and killing great numbers of rebels.

D'Bernicre exaggerates the slaughter. He doesn't mention the looting. In the words of the Reverend William Gordon, of Roxbury:

Many houses were plundered of everything valuable that could be taken away, and what could not be carried off was destroyed; looking glasses, pots, pans, etc., were broke all to pieces; doors when not fastened, sashes and windows wantonly damaged and destroyed.

Lieutenant Frederick Mackenzie, of the Royal Welsh Fusiliers, viewed these acts with concern:

I have no doubt this inflamed the Rebels, and made many of them follow us farther than they would otherwise have done. By all accounts some soldiers who staid too long in the houses were killed. . . .

Attempts were made to start more fires. One of the homes chosen was that of Deacon Joseph Adams. He had just fled, at his wife's agonized insistence. She relates:

Divers of the King's troops entered our house by bursting open the door, and three of the soldiers broke into the room in which I was confined to my bed, being scarcely able to walk from the bed to the fire, not having been to my chamber door from being delivered in child-bed to that time. One of the soldiers immediately opened my curtain with his bayonet fixed, pointing the same at my breast.

I immediately cried out, "For the Lord's sake, do not kill me!"

He replied, "Damn you!"

One that stood near said, "We will not hurt the woman, if she will go out of the house, but we will surely burn it."

I immediately arose, threw a blanket over me, and crawled into a corn-house near the door, with my infant in my arms. . . . They immediately set the house on fire, in which I had left five children [in hiding places]; but the fire was happily extinguished. . . .

The highest-ranking American officer on the field at this time was General William Heath. Because of the informal nature of the action, his control was limited. But he encouraged the men by riding often where the musket fire was hottest:

. . . I was several times greatly exposed, in particular at the high grounds at the upper end of Menotomy, and also on the plain below the meeting-house. On the latter, Dr. Joseph Warren—afterwards Major-general Warren —who kept constantly near me, and then but a few feet distant, a musket-ball from the enemy came so near his head as to strike the pin out of the hair of his earlock.

On this plain, Dr. Eliphalet Downer, in single combat with a British soldier, killed him on the spot, by thrusting him nearly through the body with his bayonet.

As the British pressed on through Cambridge, the Americans kept pursuing. Fusilier Lieutenant Mackenzie says:

. . . Altho they did not shew themselves openly in a body . . . except on the road in our rear, our men threw away their fire very inconsiderately and without being certain of its effect: this emboldened them and induced them to draw nearer, but whenever a cannon shot was fired at any considerable number, they instantly dispersed.

Daylight was beginning to fade as the weary redcoats headed for the narrow neck of the Charlestown peninsula. Some of the people of Charlestown, feeling trapped on their small triangle of land, took great alarm as the column approached and temporarily abandoned their homes. Jacob Rogers relates:

. . . it being then dark, Mr. Carey, myself, and one or two more, went into town to see if we might, with safety, proceed to our own houses. On our way, met a Mr. Hutchinson, who informed us all was then pretty quiet; that when the [British] soldiers came through the street, the officers desired the women and children to keep indoors for their safety; that they begged for drink, which the people were glad to bring them, for fear of their being ill-treated.

Mr. Carey and I proceeded to the tavern by the Town House, where the [British] officers were. All was tumult and confusion; nothing but drink called for everywhere. I stayed a few minutes, and proceeded to my own house; and finding things pretty quiet, went in search of my wife and sisters, and found them coming up the street with Capt. Adams.

On our arrival at home, we found that her brother, a youth of fourteen, was shot dead . . . by the soldiers, as he was looking out of a window. I stayed a little while to console them, and went into the main street to see if all was quiet. . . .

It was. The day's strife was over. In the opinion of Lieutenant Barker, of the King's Own:

The Rebels did not chuse to follow us to [Bunker] Hill, as they must have fought us on open ground, and that they did not like.

The trip to Concord and back had cost the British 73 killed, 174 wounded, and 26 missing. American losses were 49 killed, 39 wounded, and 5 missing. In all, perhaps 1,800 redcoats had taken part in the action. The American total is unknown, but was doubtless higher than that of the British. The fact that the Americans fought from cover was, of course, a tremendous advantage.

Military annals list few feats of endurance more remarkable than that of the redcoats of the original party. Heavily encumbered with military gear, they had, in about twenty hours, marched thirty-five or forty miles—half of the distance under savagely nerve-racking conditions.

The British did not spend the night on Bunker Hill. D'Bernicre explains:

At Charlestown . . . the Selectmen . . . sent to Lord Percy to let him know that if he would not attack the town, they would take care that the troops should not be molested, and also they would do all in their power for to get us across the ferry [to Boston]. The *Somerset* man-of-war lay there . . . and all her boats were employed first in getting over the wounded, and after them the rest of the troops.

Lieutenant Barker says:

Thus ended this expedition, which from beginning to end was as ill planned and ill executed as it was possible to be.

General Heath kept most of the American forces on the scene. They were deployed in a semicircle stretching for several miles, and their watch fires were visible to British sentries both in Charlestown and in Boston. The next day the lines were extended to shut up the neck that joined the Boston peninsula to the mainland. Thus the king's troops, who had long held American soldiers in contempt, found themselves not only vanquished by these ill-trained rustics but also (as D'Bernicre expressed it) "fairly blocked up in Boston." Even while the encirclement was being completed, Lord Percy was writing of the previous day in a private letter:

During the whole affair the rebels attacked us in a very scattered, irregular manner, but with perseverance and resolution. Nor did they ever dare to form into any regular body. Indeed, they knew too well what was proper, to do so. Whoever looks upon them as an irregular mob will find themselves much mistaken. They have men amongst them who know very well what they are about, having been employed as Rangers against the Indians and Canadians. And this country being much covered with wood, and hills, it is very advantageous for their method of fighting.

Nor are several of their men void of a spirit of enthusiasm, as we experienced yesterday, for many of them concealed themselves in houses and advanced within 10 yards to fire at me and other officers, though they were morally certain of being put to death themselves in an instant.

You may depend upon it that, as the rebels have now had time to prepare, they are determined to go through with it. Nor will the insurrection turn out so despicable as it is perhaps imagined at home.

Percy saw the situation clearly. Three weeks after Lexington and Concord, the Americans captured Fort Ticonderoga in upper New York, and in another five and a half weeks they stood up well to the British at Bunker Hill. As the war began in earnest, America developed an awareness that April 19, 1775, had been one of history's momentous days. And the same awareness would at length sweep the world. ☆

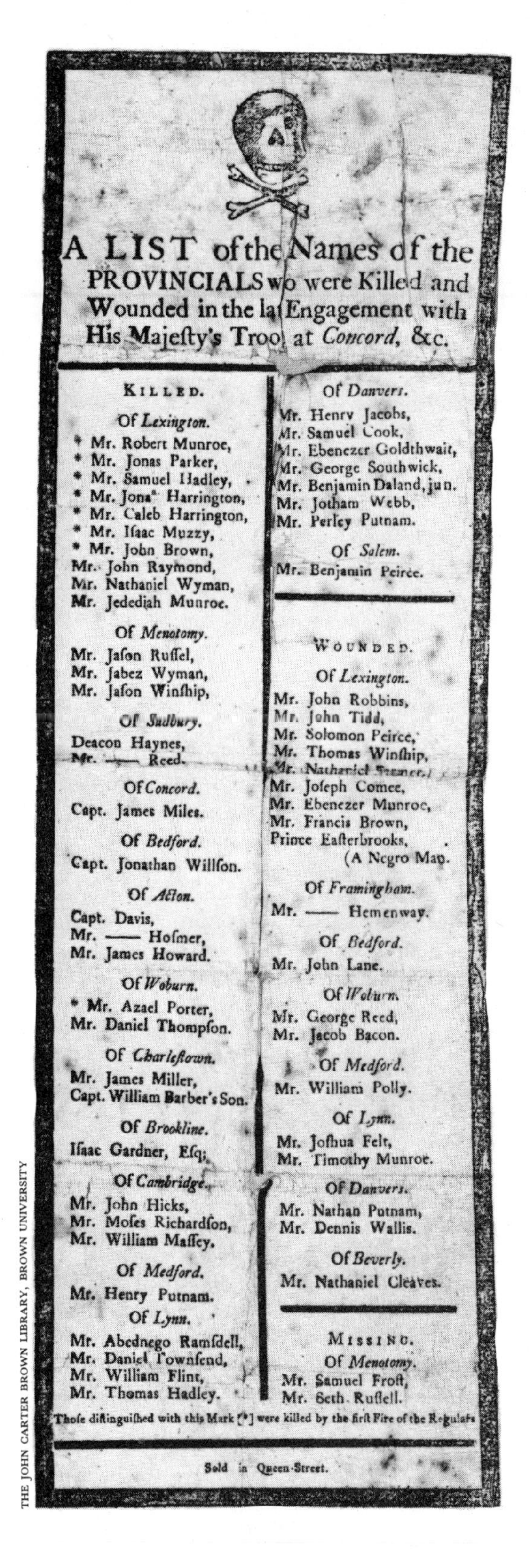

A LIST of the Names of the PROVINCIALS who were Killed and Wounded in the late Engagement with His Majeſty's Troops at *Concord*, &c.

KILLED.

Of *Lexington*.
* Mr. Robert Munroe,
* Mr. Jonas Parker,
* Mr. Samuel Hadley,
* Mr. Jona. Harrington,
* Mr. Caleb Harrington,
* Mr. Iſaac Muzzy,
* Mr. John Brown,
Mr. John Raymond,
Mr. Nathaniel Wyman,
Mr. Jedediah Munroe.

Of *Menotomy*.
Mr. Jaſon Ruſſel,
Mr. Jabez Wyman,
Mr. Jaſon Winſhip,

Of *Sudbury*.
Deacon Haynes,
Mr. —— Reed.

Of *Concord*.
Capt. James Miles.

Of *Bedford*.
Capt. Jonathan Willſon.

Of *Acton*.
Capt. Davis,
Mr. —— Hoſmer,
Mr. James Howard.

Of *Woburn*.
* Mr. Azael Porter,
Mr. Daniel Thompſon.

Of *Charleſtown*.
Mr. James Miller,
Capt. William Barber's Son.

Of *Brookline*.
Iſaac Gardner, Eſq;

Of *Cambridge*.
Mr. John Hicks,
Mr. Moſes Richardſon,
Mr. William Maſſey.

Of *Medford*.
Mr. Henry Putnam.

Of *Lynn*.
Mr. Abednego Ramſdell,
Mr. Daniel Townſend,
Mr. William Flint,
Mr. Thomas Hadley.

Of *Danvers*.
Mr. Henry Jacobs,
Mr. Samuel Cook,
Mr. Ebenezer Goldthwait,
Mr. George Southwick,
Mr. Benjamin Daland, jun.
Mr. Jotham Webb,
Mr. Perley Putnam.

Of *Salem*.
Mr. Benjamin Peirce.

WOUNDED.

Of *Lexington*.
Mr. John Robbins,
Mr. John Tidd,
Mr. Solomon Peirce,
Mr. Thomas Winſhip,
Mr. Nathaniel [illegible]
Mr. Joſeph Comee,
Mr. Ebenezer Munroe,
Mr. Francis Brown,
Prince Eaſterbrooks,
(A Negro Man.

Of *Framingham*.
Mr. —— Hemenway.

Of *Bedford*.
Mr. John Lane.

Of *Woburn*.
Mr. George Reed,
Mr. Jacob Bacon.

Of *Medford*.
Mr. William Polly.

Of *Lynn*.
Mr. Joſhua Felt,
Mr. Timothy Munroe.

Of *Danvers*.
Mr. Nathan Putnam,
Mr. Dennis Wallis.

Of *Beverly*.
Mr. Nathaniel Cleaves.

MISSING.

Of *Menotomy*.
Mr. Samuel Froſt,
Mr. Seth Ruſſell.

Thoſe diſtinguiſhed with this Mark [*] were killed by the firſt Fire of the Regulars

Sold in Queen-Street.

The opposition was still "His Majesty's" troops when this broadside came out listing the casualties of "the late Engagement"; but much blood had been spilled, and the fight for separation had begun.

The Paper Trust CONTINUED FROM PAGE 41

"as long as the repository is fireproof and the guardians faithful." In conclusion Morison urged: "But, whatever you do Mr. President, *don't* break up the collection, giving some to your children, others to Harvard, etc! Although alma mater would profit, such dispersion offends all my professorial principles."

Yet even the modest goal of preserving the Roosevelt records, instead of a complete New Deal archive, posed a problem. For one thing, the volume of White House business had mushroomed enormously. As a single instance, F.D.R.'s ability to communicate directly with the public—"My Friends"—had stimulated floods of letters to him: where Hoover had received about four hundred a day, the Roosevelt daily average in 1940 came to over four thousand. Moreover, Roosevelt was a pack rat. "I have destroyed practically nothing," he told guests at a dinner. "As a result, we have a mine for which future historians will curse me as well as praise me. It is a mine which will need to have the dross sifted from the gold."

Roosevelt's decision on how and where to locate his mine was announced after a luncheon on December 10, 1938, to which he had invited the Archivist of the United States, Robert D. W. Connor; the historian of New York State; two university presidents; the president of the League of Women Voters; such assorted literary and journalistic figures as Stuart Chase, Ernest Lindley, and Archibald MacLeish; and such past and present university professors as William E. Dodd, Frederic L. Paxson, Charles A. Beard, Helen Taft Manning, Felix Frankfurter, and Morison. The President emerged from the dining room to tell waiting reporters that after "consultation" with these luminaries, he had decided to place all of his collected papers, books, and other materials in a building to be erected, at private cost, on a portion of his Hyde Park estate that he would donate to the United States. (Eventually, he added, the entire estate would go to the federal government "to be maintained for the benefit of the public"—as in fact it has.) Within a short period of time a fund-raising corporation was established, and with a speed that later builders of Presidential libraries may well envy, the money was raised (some twenty-eight thousand individuals contributed), the building was constructed, and title was granted to the United States in mid-1940.

Roosevelt's dream of retiring to putter among his collections was never fulfilled, of course. (In typical fashion, he had jauntily refused at the December, 1938, press conference to say *when* he proposed to settle down in Hyde Park, leaving his possible third-term intentions as unclear as ever.) But the Roosevelt pattern was destined to endure. This was probably due to Truman's decision to follow his predecessor's model; it is the second man in a sequence who turns idiosyncrasy into tradition. One of Truman's administrative assistants worked with Tom L. Evans, a Kansas City businessman, to raise contributions for the building; the city of Independence gave thirteen acres for a site near Truman's home; and on July 6, 1957, the Truman Library was dedicated.

The man from Independence immediately took a hand in making it a working institution. He had an office for himself, which he occupied faithfully from nine to five, six days a week, while working on his memoirs. (To the distress of historians he sequestered large bodies of his papers for this purpose, and they have not yet been released for general use.) From time to time, according to the present assistant director of the library, he would bounce out to chat with the librarians, secretaries, and researchers at work amid the file cabinets and would often address visiting classes of schoolchildren in the library's auditorium for film displays. The staff also got accustomed to the sight of Truman leading distinguished old friends, visitors from all over the world, through his library with proprietary gusto.

By that time President Dwight Eisenhower had agreed to deposit his papers in a library-and-museum complex at Abilene. Herbert Hoover's friends, after an eightieth birthday party for him in West Branch, had launched a drive to build the Hoover Library, to which the papers of his Cabinet and Presidential years would be transferred from Stanford. And in 1955 Congress—which had allowed the government to accept the Roosevelt Library by special joint resolution—passed a general Presidential Libraries Act. Under it, the Administrator of General Services (the business arm of the federal government) could accept the papers of any President or former President, as well as "any land, buildings, and equipment offered as a gift to the United States for the purposes of creating a Presidential archival depository," and could likewise, if need be, agree to operate such a depository even if title to the property remained with some state, political subdivision, foundation, or institution.

Even before the tragically abrupt end of the Kennedy administration, plans were afoot for the Kennedy Library, and the subject of where to locate the Johnson Library was also on the White House staff agenda long before 1968. Both Presidents had initiated record-keeping and record-compiling programs within Executive agencies, the first rough sketches for the historical portraits of their periods of tenure.

A foundation was set up in 1969 to select a site for a library for President Nixon in southern California. The exact location (which the President will have to approve) is a matter not only of local pride but of dollars and cents. For like all the other libraries this one will bring tourists, motels and restaurants to shelter and nourish them, and bulldozers leaving ribbons of concrete highway trailing behind them—all developments of much interest to real-estate promoters. And on some date in 1973 or 1977 the Nixon papers, like those of every President before him since Franklin Roosevelt, will be truckloaded (at government expense) to the waiting library or to a federal warehouse if the library is not yet completed. The haul will include not only the tiny percentage of papers actually originated by the President and signed by him, but all others in his files. Carbon copies of most of them will be available in the agencies that sent the originals—but it is conceivable that the President might, wittingly or not, take with him the lone copy of some document vitally needed by his successor. [See "How Harding Saved the Versailles Treaty" in the December, 1968, issue of AMERICAN HERITAGE.]

For several years thereafter, government-paid archivists will sort, label, catalogue, index, and otherwise tame the paper wilderness and provide it with signposts and pathways for historical explorers. Meanwhile, the Nixon Library —and other Presidential libraries which may have been set up by then—will continue to grow by accession. Its director will, like his colleagues in charge of the existing libraries, want to make his library a center for study of the entire era of "his" President. He will try to collect papers—and at least tape-recorded oral history interviews—from members of the Cabinet, heads of Executive agencies (like the FCC or OEO), unofficial but major advisers and close friends, party committeemen, deputy and assistant-deputy officials, key legislators, journalists, associates of pre-Presidential years, and so on down the line to minor types, the water-bucket carriers and rubdown specialists of the Presidential team.

Finally the Nixon Library will be a mature, fully functioning archive, like the six that precede it in time—and, perhaps, like those to come after it, if post-Nixon Presidents do not return to the casual records-disposal practices of an earlier day.

At that point, it would appear, the historians should have cause to rejoice. The key American records—manuscripts, films, and tapes—of the central decades of the twentieth century will be neatly on file in protected surroundings, instead of laid up in attics "where moth and rust doth corrupt, and where thieves break through." This year, presumably, the Roosevelt and Truman libraries (respectively in their third and second decades of use) are already helping to unravel such mysteries as what happened at Yalta and Potsdam, how much influence brain trusters and cronies had in domestic policies, and who planted the seeds of "containment." By 1981, therefore, the Eisenhower, Kennedy, and Johnson libraries may be expected to make an open book of equally gnarled questions: the U-2 flights, the Bay of Pigs affair, and Vietnam. And so the Presidential-library system will stand vindicated and blessed by scholarship.

Alas, as even the directors of the libraries themselves are aware, the scenario does not read so smoothly. For there are severe limitations on the use of the Presidential papers now, and unless they are overcome, they may leave tomorrow's historians, despite the archival machinery at their disposal, even more frustrated than yesterday's, who had to grope their uncertain way to long-lost trunks full of mildewing papers.

First of all, since the outbreak of World War II, a vast proportion of the White House files originating in the State Department and the War and Navy (and later Defense) departments have been classified to protect national security. Ten, twenty, and even thirty years after the events with which they deal, their SECRET and TOP SECRET stamps remain as binding as ever. Until they are officially reviewed and declassified—a process compared to which glaciers sprint—they are either entirely closed to scholars or can be studied only under severe reservations. The user must be fingerprinted and his security checked; he must swear that he does not belong to any of a list of subversive organizations; his notes and manuscript must be reviewed by State and/or Defense officials, a process that may take months. Nor is there any court of appeal.

Although the entire classification system (except for Atomic Energy Commission materials, which are classified by statute) rests on Executive Order, a retired President may not disclose the contents of secret papers—even those that he himself wrote. Lyndon Johnson, it is known, had a special team of Defense Department specialists examine his files after he left office, in the hope that they might authorize the speedy release of information that he believes is necessary to understand his actions. Their almost predictable answer was No.

In addition to the papers closed for security reasons, there is another substantial body of material kept from researchers in the libraries. This comprises the communications that, in the language of an official NARS handout for researchers, contain statements "which may be used to injure, embarrass or harass any living person," or which were "obviously made in confidence," or which "relate strictly to a person's private, family or business affairs." The reason for the policy is clear. Many of the papers received by the President and his associates unsparingly discuss—often on the basis of rumor and gossip—the private fragilities of public men. NARS believes that the neuroses, divorces, diseases, and private financial pressures of key legislators or potential appointees to office are not public matters unless there is clear proof that they affect public performance. Moreover, thousands of letters to the President come from ordinary citizens who pour out their personal agonies in detail to an unknown man whom they see as a superfather. A blackmailer could function briskly simply by frequenting the libraries and using these files.

It is thus a custom for the library staffs to review incoming collections and "close" materials that fall within these categories. Periodically they go over them anew, with a list of recent obituaries at hand, and "open" those items dealing with individuals whom death has put beyond the sting of scandal. (Donors may, however, require that their papers be closed for long periods of time after their death or that of people mentioned in them.) At best, this practice is a compromise between the public's right to know and the individual's right to privacy. And like any compromise it yields incomplete satisfaction to both parties.

Yet no scholar can reasonably complain about protecting the human rights of those who serve the nation in government posts and those who correspond with them. Nor are scholars unwilling to help protect the nation from harm through premature revelations: private agreements with heads of foreign powers, reports on the military preparedness of allies, intelligence estimates that name the source of their information. But many responsible historians do resent what James MacGregor Burns, a distinguished biographer of Franklin D. Roosevelt, calls "the absurd overkill of the present restrictions." Burns knows whereof he speaks. He has had to run the gauntlet of security clearance in order to see documents that are now twenty-five years old at a minimum.

Furthermore, the restrictive tendency of the classifying authorities appears to be increasing with time. The State Department used to publish its volumes of diplomatic documents, entitled *Foreign Relations of the United States*, some fifteen years after the events they recorded. The time lag is now nearing thirty years. Perhaps the reason lies not only in secrecy but in the volume of the materials and in staff and budget limitations. But whatever the reason, a middle-aged historian of recent foreign affairs cannot entertain much hope of getting a wholly accurate story in his lifetime. Critics of the security policy also say that it reflects bureaucratic caution as much as it does prudence. The "secrets" themselves are rarely very potent. Many have been revealed in memoirs. Most date rather quickly. The total classified record, Burns notes, "consists of millions of items, none very crucial in itself." The need for secrecy "after a span of a few years," he concludes, "is largely a myth."

Other historians who deal in primary sources are disturbed at excessive respect for the confidentiality of personal interchanges among the mighty. First, they argue, there is always the possibility that a personal matter—the actual illness of Woodrow Wilson in 1919; the possible illness of Franklin D. Roosevelt in early 1945; the approaching madness of James Forrestal, first Secretary of Defense, in 1949—may be the urgently needed key to comprehending a historical development. Furthermore, the current policy places a tremendous burden on the discretion of the library officials. They must comb the materials and, when a letter contains both public and private materials, make the tricky judgment of which element predominates. They may become overcautious. Or one of them may, through long association with a given President's history, tend toward becoming a keeper of the flame, unwilling to jeopardize "his" man's reputation by putting materials in the hands of a known critic.

Moreover, historians do not get an equal shot at the record. It does not remain totally veiled during the years when it is officially closed. Presidents, generals, Cabinet members, White House aides, and staff members often rush to their typewriters to write reminiscences that will make themselves presentable in the history books. They send assistants and clerks ruffling through their papers, often still in official files. They give inside accounts to favored book-writing reporters. In addition, the State and Defense departments (as well as other federal agencies) have official historians who have the insider's clear track, not only to files but, more importantly, to frequent, familiar, and confidential interviews with the historical actors themselves. The viewpoints that dominate these official histories become in essence those of the commissioning agencies.

Piecemeal, therefore, a version of the recent past, tailored to official and individual vanity, emerges. But the independent historian or journalist, who is most likely to have the training and the perspective to create a useful chronicle and to interpret it objectively, remains shut out from this favored group until a generation has passed. The long-run cost, argue Burns and Herbert Feis, the diplomatic historian, is great. If knowledge of history is to be helpful to people and their leaders, it must be timely. Against the need for security and privacy there stand the claims of the nation, which cannot afford to make its archives, Feis says, like those of totalitarian states —"mortuaries which only licensed embalmers . . . are allowed to enter." And, too, he adds, the world has a claim on the keepers of the record. In this era of tragic national behavior, "greater openness, by all governments, might improve the health of the international community by nurturing it on the whole truth, even if it tastes bitter." Burns and Feis do not argue that restrictions should be abandoned, but only that the record should be opened much more quickly—Burns suggests about eight years after it is made. The Presidential libraries are not specifically blamed for "privileged history" but for involuntarily sharing in the system that creates it.

To such remonstrances the various directors of the Presidential libraries, past and present, have a variety of answers. The first is that they must work within the "givens" of the system. One of these is that, while Presidents may willingly deposit their records in special libraries built to house them, in the foreseeable future there is no likelihood of compelling former Chief Executives to relinquish the papers to public scrutiny on any terms but their own. Even if a law should be passed making the White House files public documents, a President would be within his rights in sifting out exclusively private papers for removal. If NARS officials challenged his judgment on what was purely personal matter, the resulting contests could, in the words of one of them, keep "a whole battery of lawyers busy" for a long time.

Moreover, to insist that anything in the White House's incoming mailbag ought to be given to the populace for early inspection would chill frankness. As former Truman administrative assistant David Lloyd once wrote, few men would write to a President in confidence and few Presidents would put their private thoughts on paper if the end of the term was a signal for disclosure. "And as a consequence, the ability of the President to function as an independent officer of the Government would be curtailed, if not crippled. . . ." It is unquestionably true that a good public servant must be allowed to suggest outrageously unpopular courses of action—if only for discussion—without being pilloried for it soon thereafter. (Contemporary public men already worry considerably in crisis conferences about indiscreet colleagues who may already have contracts for their memoirs in hand.)

If the President exerts his right to put his papers in a marble monument built by hometown friends in a location far from traditional seats of learning, the conscientious archivist has no choice but to follow them there, care for them, and display them under whatever conditions are allowed. If he is a truly hard-working archivist—as all the Presidential library directors are—he will urge the President's co-workers also to deposit their papers there. He is not likely to get such deposits without being able to give assurances that the public will not soon be let into the donor's inner life; as the mediator between the future historian and the gun-shy subjects of history, his first rule of operation is to get the material preserved. The Presidential libraries have actually hastened a policy of accumulation that would ordinarily have taken generations.

The papers of the First Ladies, too, are an important source of history hitherto ignored, before they became part of Presidential-library collections. In the case of Eleanor Roosevelt, her own independent career generated so large a collection that it is being moved into a new wing of the Roosevelt Library, to be opened in 1971 and to become in itself an important center for the study of the politics, social problems, and philanthropic work of her time.

Galling as the policy of restriction is, the library spokesmen note that a larger amount of Presidential material is open than ever before, and open to all comers, critical or not. (The only entrance test for access to unclassified material is a statement of some reasonable purpose.) One former director of the Roosevelt Library enjoyed pointing out that Roosevelt's papers were processed and opened for use in 1950, five years after the President's death. Eighty-five per cent of the material, he declared, was open to inspection. Yet only *three* years before, in 1947, the Library of Congress had proudly opened a large collection of Abraham Lincoln papers that had been closed until then by the desire of the donor, Lincoln's son. The papers of both Presidents Adams were not available for public use until the middle 1960's. Other Presidential papers lay hidden for decades.

The fact is that the historians are succumbing, like others in modern times, to a revolution of rising expectations. More is available to them than ever before, and their appetite grows by what it feeds on. The archivists claim that they encourage rather than deplore this hunger. Each library proudly points to the number of "researcher visits" it experiences each year (around a thousand each for the Roosevelt and Truman libraries from July 1, 1969, to June 30, 1970) and to the growing list of books, articles, and dissertations founded primarily on its materials.

The Truman Library happily cooperates with a privately created and financed nonprofit organization, the Harry S. Truman Library Institute for National and International Affairs, which aims to provide grants-in-aid to scholars using the library, to foster publications based on its materials, and to sponsor conferences on topics stemming from developments of the Truman period. This institute may be a model for other libraries. Former President Johnson is known to hope that his library will also sponsor seminars on social, environmental, and economic problems, which will draw together the experts and the documents. The museum directors, too, attempt to keep their materials on display in a manner that educates as well as attracts the public.

Such activities are a long way from the caginess and record-hugging attributed to the libraries by some critics. But, strangely, the collecting energies of the directors raise some other disturbing reflections. It is possible that the sheer glut of material may defeat historians to come. The information explosion threatens to bury them in documentation. Clicking Xerox machines, microfilm cameras, and whirling tape reels all proliferate information. In point of fact, even if all future Presidents were compelled to leave their official records in Washington, it would be necessary to build completely new repositories to hold them, simply because of the multiplying size of the Executive Department and because its officials, like those of all Washington, are pouring out a rising flood of paper. The National Archives building itself long ago became inadequate as the sole reservoir. In 1950 a program of decentralization was put in motion, designed to set up new Federal Records Centers throughout the country. There are now fifteen of them, housing 10.8 million cubic feet of records. And the torrent is not abating.

But the wrenching irony is that not all of this is gold for history. The duplicating machines immeasurably encourage the preservation of routine papers. And two other inventions—the telephone and the jet airplane—nibble away at the materials of major significance. When Abraham Lincoln wished to say something to General Grant in Virginia, he had to send a telegram or write a note. But when Lyndon Johnson felt the need to speak to General Westmoreland, he had only to pick up the telephone to Saigon—or to fly there himself, or have the General fly to Washington, in a matter of hours. And such face-to-face or over-the-wire conferences may never be recorded.

A certain amount of the crucial business of history has always been preserved only in the memory of those who transacted it. The size and importance of that "unrecorded record" is now growing. This is why contemporary Presidential libraries are undertaking extensive interview programs. The Kennedy Library, for example, already has taped and transcribed about five hundred interviews with such key Kennedy men as Dean Rusk, Robert McNamara, McGeorge Bundy, and Pierre Salinger and with a host of others who knew the President—a cast of great variety, including men like U Thant, Richard Cardinal Cushing, and John Glenn. (Such transcripts are held under the same rules of confidentiality that apply to written materials.)

Oral history fills gaps in the written records. But is it possible to interpret them, with the gaps filled, or does their overpowering massiveness make them impenetrable? True, dazzling technical means of storage and retrieval of information are available. Given the investment of enough money and time, it is perfectly feasible that all Presidential or other documents can be "read" and "memorized" by computers before being microfilmed and filed. Then a historian may be able to give an electronic command to some robot Clio, such as: "Bring me all the materials on assistance programs to rural areas in Southeast Asia from 1958 to 1970." But what will he do when she faithfully beeps, rumbles, and neatly prints out fifty thousand references on the topic. Will useful synthesis then be possible?

Such a question gets to the root of what history is all about. Modern "scientific" history was born less than a century ago. It aimed to be more than—or at least different from—philosophy and literature. It rested on the happy nineteenth-century assumption that there was a discernible pattern, coherence, and direction in the affairs of humanity—discernible, that is, when the whole record was collected and scanned. The historians were like Roman soothsayers reading the entrails of a sacred beast. The beast was the past. And he who knew the past, in a sense, knew the future as well.

But what will happen when the record is so gigantic as to become an abstraction like infinity itself? Then the Presidential libraries, like all contemporary research libraries, may remain as husks without kernels, like the cathedrals after the high point of the Age of Christianity. They will be souvenirs of time past, but not the active centers of a civilization's faith.

Their long, loaded shelves may only increase the perplexity of modern man, who, even without a glut of records, is already likely to find history uncomforting and incomprehensible. ☆

At War with the Stars and Stripes CONTINUED FROM PAGE 64

had wide interests and horizons. We were, many of us, fresh from the New Deal years, and some of the sociological thinking for the little man (temporarily called the enlisted man) pervaded the reporting, not only of staff members but of letter writers and poets.

Stars and Stripes achieved a historical place because it was an altogether human paper; it became the printed record of the emotions and passions of its readers. Had it been up to some of the generals and commands, especially the base sections in the rear, *Stars and Stripes* would have been reduced to little more than an Army house organ. Some of the brass considered it only a training manual, publicity release, or hot potato, and seldom just a newspaper.

Whenever a particular command wanted to disavow disputes in the paper, they would issue an order making the paper "unofficial." Nobody could logically explain how a newspaper run by sergeants, administered by captains and colonels, in turn drawing pay from the Army, could be unofficial. The other method of buck-passing by the Army was to keep shifting the command echelon above; an edition might be under a base section, special services, information and education, or Allied Force Headquarters itself.

From the Army's point of view—except for the brief existence of *Stars and Stripes* in World War I—there was no tradition of untrammelled expression; indeed, that was the antithesis of military discipline and unquestioning conformity. The serious *Stars and Stripes* editors were always aware of this apparently irreconcilable conflict. Yet they strove to turn the paper into the voice of men—like themselves—temporarily in uniform, to deliver the news professionally and idealistically, to reflect ideas under stress and our postwar aspirations.

The Second World War multiplied battles and ideals all over the globe. By contrast, the Vietnam folly has diminished the United States in the eyes of even those peoples who once were freed by American soldiers. Correspondents and other observers caught up in wars past and present must still sit upon the ground and talk and write without sentiment of dictators and comrades; of the blacks and whites of conscience peering through the smoke; above all, of the need to escalate—in Asia and elsewhere—not the battles, but the ideals.

Herbert Mitgang is on the editorial board of the New York Times. *A member of the Society of American Historians, he has written and edited books in several fields, including* Abraham Lincoln: A Press Portrait, The Letters of Carl Sandburg, The Man Who Rode the Tiger, *and* Civilians Under Arms.

The Old Vets

CONTINUED FROM PAGE 57

Last of all, I remember George Jackson, colored, who before the War was employed by my maternal grandfather, proprietor of the town's largest livery stable. In 1863, when the Commonwealth of Massachusetts adopted legislation legalizing the recruiting of Negro regiments, George went off to the War. Some time after, his name appeared among those of men killed or missing in action. One evening my grandmother was sitting in the parlor of her Main Street home, thinking sadly of faithful George, of whom the family had been fond. The house stood but ten or fifteen feet back from the sidewalk with no hedge or fence between. As was customary, the shades were not drawn. Suddenly George's face appeared at one of the windows. Taken by surprise, for a moment my grandmother did not know whether the face at the window was an apparition or that of the real George—which, of course, it was.

In the summer of 1910 the Western Massachusetts Grand Army Association held its eighteenth annual field day at the Mount Sugarloaf State Reservation in South Deerfield. Though the Veterans came from Springfield, Holyoke, Northampton, Greenfield, North Adams, Turners Falls, Shelburne Falls, Orange, Amherst, and many other western Massachusetts towns, there were present hardly more than two hundred. By this time the Veterans were being referred to, especially when assembled in a body, as the "Old Vets," a term that was a combination of tolerance and affection.

By 1910 there were so few of the Old Vets in our city who could march the mile to the cemetery on Decoration Day, that they were provided with transportation in the open automobiles of the period. Their place behind the band that now led the procession was taken by those who in 1898 had fought in Cuba in the less glorious war with Spain.

Certainly with respect to the G.A.R. it was true that old soldiers "just fade away." Each succeeding May 30 those Veterans who rode in the annual parade were fewer in number; but this was so in accord with the immutable laws of nature that it almost passed unnoticed—until one day the community awoke to the fact that Alfonso Witherell was the only Civil War Veteran still living in our city. He had long since hung up his mailbag but was still a familiar figure on Main Street. Then, on February 7, 1944, at the age of one hundred years, eight months, and twenty days, Alfonso Witherell, the last of the Old Vets, answered his final roll call.

A retired college teacher, Mr. Dewey now lives in Los Angeles, where he is writing his memoirs.

Of Noble Warriors...

CONTINUED FROM PAGE 53

slender, and as flexible as the stem of a river-flag—waving hair of a deep chestnut, twisted up into a shining braid on the snowy neck; and eyes—ah, those eyes!—they were languishing, brilliant, and of an intense and dazzling violet—that tint which the summer sky wears when the purple of the sunset dashes against the blue. . . . As she stood there in the moonlight, keeping time with her slipper to the strains of the "Mocking Bird," I thought she was some fairy—not a girl of flesh and blood!

Mordaunt has sworn vengeance against his erstwhile friend, Fenwick, who had earlier abducted Mordaunt's wife. Fenwick had kept his captive at Elm Cottage in the wilderness; there she had borne Mordaunt's son, who was promptly spirited away by Fenwick, and there she lived in madness for many years. She was cared for by her "keeper," Mrs. Parkins, and at the last, just before her death, by her beautiful young cousin, Violet Grafton—Heroine Number Two. Surry begins to learn the tragic story when he stumbles on the cottage and seeks shelter for the night. Mordaunt is determined to avenge his wife and to protect Violet from the foul clutches of the evil Fenwick.

As if this were not enough to keep everyone busy, Surry and Mordaunt also find time to pursue their military careers, fighting in the battles of First Manassas and Chancellorsville, receiving rapid promotions, and covering themselves with glory.

The plots unfold in a manner that must have gratified the lady readers. May and Philip are united when Baskerville releases her from her promise. With the sound of artillery fire in the distance, the lovers pledge their devotion fervently, but with Victorian propriety:

> Yet who shall dare to laugh at the spectacle of a proud and beautiful girl, long fettered by a hateful contract, shuddering at a loathsome union with a man she despises—who shall laugh when she gives way to her heart, and, falling weak and overcome into the arms of one who has loved her long and dearly, murmurs, "Take charge of my poor life—direct my fate—I have loved, and love you only!"

Later, Mordaunt is reunited with his long-lost son, who appears from the blue. Learning that Fenwick now holds the lovely Violet prisoner, Mordaunt pursues him to Elm Cottage, where his wife had died long before. One would expect that Mordaunt has earned the right to do Fenwick in, but that unworthy dies in an even more melodramatic way. Achmed, Mordaunt's handsome young Arab servant, who has cherished a hopeless passion for Violet, dashes in and stabs Fenwick to the heart, an organ one would not have thought he possessed. In his dying throes, shouting words of implacable hate, Fenwick fires his pistol, wounds Achmed, clutches the air, foams at the mouth, and falls dead. The scene's finale must have caused the readers' tears to fall like rain:

> Dragging himself along, Achmed reached her [Violet's] feet, and, taking one of her hands, pressed it closely to his lips, murmuring some faint words . . . in his native tongue.
>
> "He says he is happy for he dies for you!" exclaimed the deep voice of Mordaunt, as he stood with arms folded across his heaving bosom.

And so Cooke has given his readers daring heroes, chaste and lovely heroines, a dastardly villain, incessant action both on and off the field of battle, and love both pure and lustful.

Today, one is likely to read these novels with mixed feelings of interest, frustration, and incredulity. It is undeniably interesting to read the authors' accounts of the battles in which they took part and their impressions of the military leaders with whom they rode and fought. It is also frustrating, for they were far too mindful of their "delicate" readers to give undiluted descriptions of the actualities of battle. Cooke, in particular, seems to have regarded the war, at least in retrospect, as a glorious adventure. Speaking through his hero, he says:

> I often look back now to those days with a longing desire to live them over again. . . . It was a life all excitement and romance which we lived at that epoch—days of fighting, of incident, of adventure; nights of hasty slumber, in rude bivouac under the forest trees, or of long, confidential talks by the smouldering campfires. . . .

Occasionally, though, a glimpse of truth forces its way into his pages. Surry does not fight at Sharpsburg but sees the battlefield just after the fighting has ended:

> Before me was a picturesque valley, hemmed in upon the east by the wooded ramparts of the South Mountain, and traversed by the winding current of the Antietam . . . a landscape which must have been charming only the day before.
>
> Now it was torn, dismantled, and swept bare by the besom of war. All day the opposing battalions had charged backward and forward through those smiling fields; from behind those peaceful farm-houses, now crowded with the dead and wounded, sharpshooters had delivered their hot fire; the corn was trampled under-foot; the ground ploughed up with shot and shell; the whole face of nature desolate.

More often, however, as with Nichols, the romanticist in Cooke remains firmly in control over the realist.

But to the modern reader incredulity is the feeling that prevails as one closes these Civil War best sellers, these hodgepodges of war story, soap opera, and Gothic thriller. What an appetite our ancestors must have had for unreality!

Irene M. Patten is a New Englander who has taught English in secondary schools in Maine and Massachusetts.

POSTSCRIPTS TO HISTORY

RIGHT FACE

Dr. Gilbert Highet, long the noted Anthon Professor of Latin at Columbia University, recently wrote us, saying:

I was looking at some old furniture in East Hampton when I remembered something once told me by an American officer who heard me speak at West Point. . . . He said that you could always tell the date of a piece of nineteenth-century furniture if it had the American eagle on it, because if the country had been at war when the piece was made, the eagle was looking to the side in which it held the lightning bolts, and if we were at peace, it had its head turned to the side of the olive branch. Is there any truth to this?

Miss Sarah B. Sherrill of *Antiques* magazine was kind enough to check into this possibility of dating old furniture and found it was—perhaps unfortunately for buffs—a myth. Which way the eagle faced, she discovered, "depended on the whim of the artist." Indeed, artists, we also ascertained, not only faced their

American eagle correctly posed

eagles to the left or right without a war-or-peace theory in mind, but also exchanged the lightning bolts and olive branch from one claw to another for no discernible reason. Until President Harry S. Truman decreed otherwise in 1945, the President's seal, coat of arms, and flag carried the eagle facing the bolts in its left talon. This was changed by executive order so that the eagle looks to its right—the position of honor in heraldry. It thus now faces the talon holding the olive branch. The eagle on our cover, a wood carving dated 1840, is hence wrong: it has no olive branch at all.

AMEN

George L. Howe, a contributor to this magazine in the past and a long-time subscriber, took a look at the gravestone rubbings by Avon Neal and Ann Parker in our August, 1970, issue ("Graven Images: Sermons in Stones") and was prompted to try to identify an old epitaph he had often seen quoted: "Young to the pulpit did he get, / And seventy-two years in't did he sweat."

As Mr. Howe puts it, "Even in that sudorific age, seventy-two years must have come close to the record for clerical perspiration." He believes he found the holder of said record in the *Biographical Dictionary* compiled in 1809 by John Eliot, corresponding secretary of the Massachusetts Historical Society. The man who fits the bill, Mr. Howe says, is the Reverend John Higginson, who was born in England in 1616 and came to the New World when he was twelve. The son of a minister, Higginson assisted the pastor of Guilford, Connecticut, from 1643 to 1659, when he moved to his father's church in Salem, Massachusetts. He was ordained its pastor in 1660 and died at the age of ninety-two in 1708.

Assuming that he preached for seventy-two years, as per the epitaph, Mr. Howe surmises that this man of God must have been twenty years old at the time of his first sermon, sometime in 1636. That, he says, "doesn't seem an improbably early age for his sweating to have begun."

. . . AND A MAID

The indefatigable Mr. Howe also recalls another great epitaph, which will perhaps amuse the Latin scholars among our readers. It is a parody by Longfellow of the one Dr. Samuel Johnson composed for Oliver Goldsmith: "*Nullum quod tetigit non ornavit.*" Longfellow called his, "Epitaph on a Maid of All Work:"

Hic jacet ancilla
Quae omnia egit;
Et nihil tetigit
Quod non fregit.

"It has been stylish, even during his lifetime, to laugh at Longfellow as a linguist," concludes Mr. Howe, "but I think that translating 'maid of all work' as '*ancilla quae omnia egit*' is a *tour de force* that Dean Swift himself could not have excelled."

NEVER ASK A LADY . . .

We were purposely vague about the year of birth of Willa Cather in introducing the article she wrote about the fortieth anniversary of Brownville, Nebraska, in the October, 1970, issue ("Ghost Town on the River"). However, Virginia Faulkner, editor of the University of Nebraska Press, insists that there is "no uncertainty" at all about the birth date; it was December 7, 1873:

Miss Cather started fudging on her age when she began to be well known as a novelist, and for years all sources listed her as born in 1876. But as long ago as 1951 Mildred Bennett, in *The World of Willa Cather*, proved incontrovertibly that 1873 was the year (birth certificate, letter from Charles Cather announcing the event, and family Bible). The family Bible is now in the restored Cather home in Red Cloud, and on the birth-record page one can see that Miss Cather made a game attempt to change Wilella to Willa and 1873 to 1876. All our Cather publications and most recent scholarship in the field give the date correctly, and gradually standard reference works are making the correction, but the wrong date is still given in a flock of them. Perhaps when the Cather centennial is celebrated in 1973 they'll pull up their socks.

SOLD OUT

After 194 years the federal government

has formally gone out of the silver business. During most of that time the U.S. Treasury had purchased only the silver it needed to mint coins, but it began to stockpile the metal in 1934 to bolster the depressed mining industry. Then, with the increase in photographic and other industrial uses after World War II, the Treasury turned seller in an effort to keep the price of silver down, so that its own coins would not become more valuable to melt down than to use as money. Since the phasing out of most silver coins and their replacement by lead-colored "sandwiches" of nickel and copper, the Treasury's role as a holder or seller of silver has disappeared. Last October it auctioned off its last marketable silver, 1.5 million ounces, at $1.84 per ounce. (The Treasury still has thirty-five million unrefined ounces left; they are earmarked for Eisenhower silver dollars.) With bimetallism for all intents and purposes now a dead issue, one Treasury official commented that "William Jennings Bryan must be spinning in his grave."

PARSON WEEMS'S LAW

Governments pass laws constantly, but the only ones with any lasting force are those unofficial ones provided us by Newton, Gresham, Acton, Parkinson, and others like them who have observed the basic cussedness of things. In the business of history we have a little rule of this kind that is (or ought to be) known as Parson Weems's Law. It has given us Washington and the cherry tree, Pilgrims jumping onto Plymouth Rock, young Lincoln courting Ann Rutledge, the unstained innocence of Sacco and Vanzetti—but enough examples. Let us state the law:

Historical fancy is more persistent than historical fact.

The law at work is demonstrated, to the deep regret of the editors of our new *American Heritage History of the 20's and 30's*, on page 321 of that book, in the account of President Franklin Roosevelt's attempt to "pack" the Supreme Court. The book states that one of the Court's then members, Justice Pierce Butler, of Minnesota, "had failed in constitutional law at college." That was the fancy circulated at the time of the battle over "nine old men" who were supposed to be impeding justice, right, reform, and All That Is Good. A recent work of erudition on Justices of the Court perpetuates the error and was routinely consulted on the point by our book's checker.

Now, however, we hear from the late Justice's indignant daughter, Mrs. Edward K. Dunn, of Baltimore, who possesses a transcript of his grades at Carleton College in Minnesota. In 1887–88, his senior year, he was given a mark of 7.6 (on a scale of 10) in constitutional law, which is clearly passing. We apologize to Mrs. Dunn and assure her that any future editions of the book will be corrected. But we cannot promise that, even in this carefully checked magazine, Parson Weems will not strike again.

LAST STOP

After nearly a decade of litigation the town of Kennesaw (originally humble Big Shanty), Georgia, has finally won back for good a picturesque locomotive that was stolen from there by Union soldiers 109 years ago. The engine, known as the *General*, and three boxcars were taken by James J. Andrews, an espionage agent, and nineteen federal soldiers in disguise while the train was stopped at Kennesaw for a breakfast break on April 12, 1862. The Northerners planned to run the train to Chattanooga, then the objective of a Union Army offensive, and, by burning bridges on the way, hoped to seal that city off from Confederate forces to the south and east. Andrews and his men never made it, however. The train crew bolted from the breakfast table as their train pulled away and gave chase first on foot and then in commandeered locomotives. Eight hours and eighty-seven miles later, after many hairbreadth episodes twice glorified in movies, the *General* ran out of steam. Andrews and the Union men hid in the woods, but all were rounded up within a week and he and seven others were executed. The *General* returned to serve the southern cause and survived the Battle of Atlanta, though in a badly battered shape. In 1870 her owner, the Georgia Railroad, leased the engine to the newly formed Western & Atlantic Railroad, which converted her from a wood burner to a coal burner. After that line was acquired by the Nashville, Chattanooga & St. Louis Railroad in 1890, the *General* was spotted by an enterprising photographer sitting amid the weeds on a siding at Vining's, Georgia. The NC & StL restored the engine in her W & A livery and then put her on display under the train shed of Chattanooga's Union Station. There she rested, except for brief excursions to such fairs as the Columbian Exposition in Chicago, until the Louisville & Nashville Railroad absorbed the NC & StL in the late 1950's. Since Chattanooga citizens were in no mood to have their venerated locomotive moved out of state, Louisville & Nashville officials resorted to kidnapping to use the engine in a planned centennial re-enactment of her Civil War escapade. Early in June, 1961, the wire fence surrounding the *General* was cut, and the engine, covered with canvas, was pulled from the train shed across a specially laid sixty feet of track to the railroad's main line. She was then hoisted aboard a flatcar and sped the next day to Louisville, where the engine was converted anew, this time to an oil burner. On February 7, 1962, the *General* operated under her own power for the first time since 1914 and two months later performed handily in the centennial celebration, followed by a nationwide tour. When the railroad then announced its intention to deposit the engine at Kennesaw, the already-irate city of Chattanooga took the matter to court, contending that the *General* was its "charitable trust." The suit was finally settled this past November by the U.S. Supreme Court, which let stand a lower court ruling that said the railroad could take the engine anywhere it wished.

DOUGLAS WORNOM

The restored General *nearing the Hell Gate Bridge, New York, 1964, with a period combine*

T.R.
on the Writing of History

CULVER PICTURES

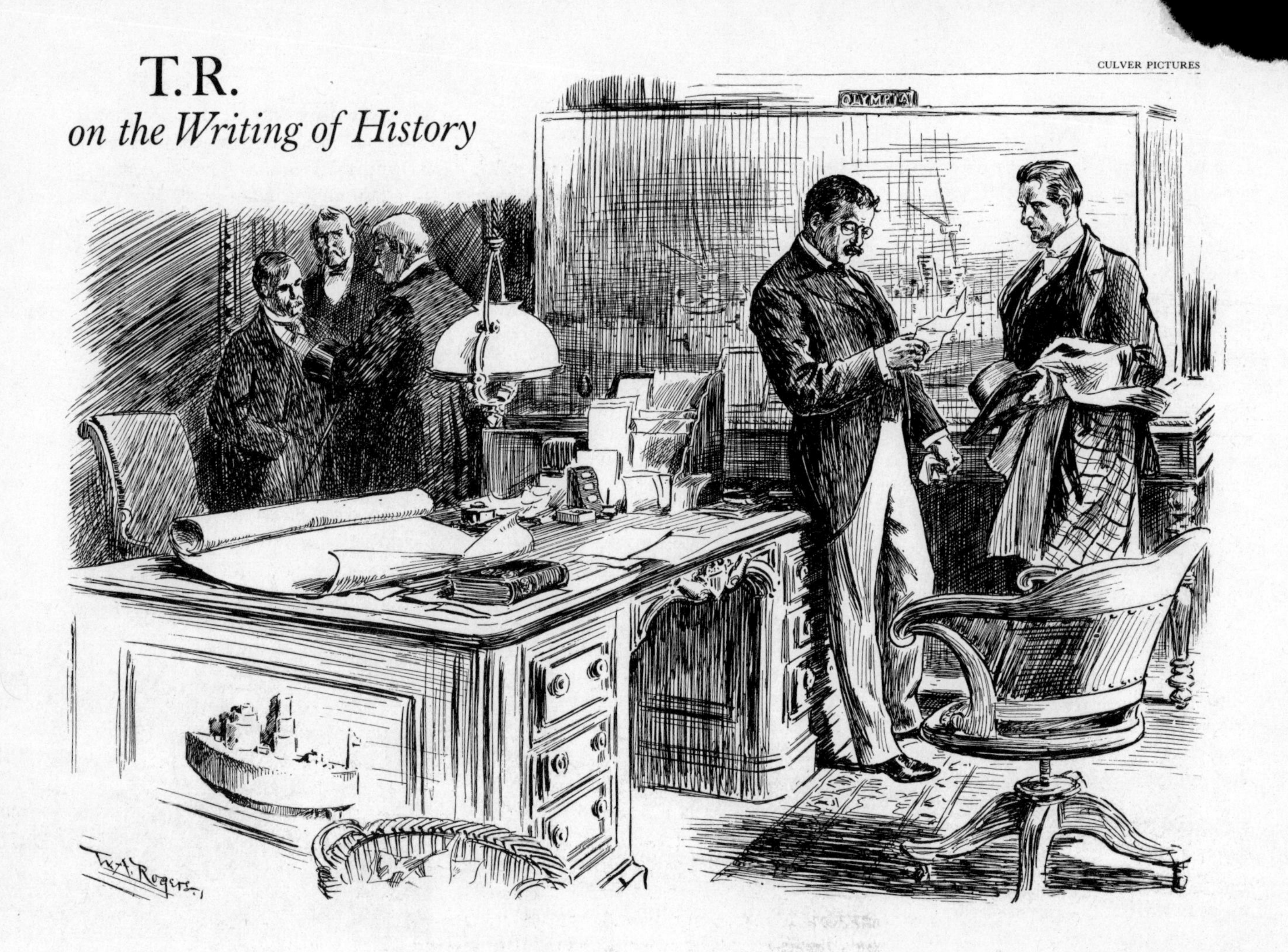

Few of our thirty-seven Presidents have been highly gifted with literary talent; of those few, fewer had the time or the patience to sit down and deliberately write books. Theodore Roosevelt, who was among the most gifted, also crammed into his "strenuous" life more nonliterary activity than perhaps any other President. Yet somehow, in a career of nearly forty years, he managed to produce more than twenty published books—histories, biographies, collections of essays, accounts of hunting expeditions, an autobiography. As on every other topic, Roosevelt had very definite ideas about writing, especially the writing of history. In the midst of a busy day at the White House in January, 1904, he took a few minutes to dictate a letter to British historian Sir George Trevelyan that included this passage:*

We have a preposterous little organization called I think the American Historical Association, which, when I was just out of Harvard and very ignorant, I joined. [Time softened T.R.'s opinion: he himself became president of the association in 1912.] Fortunately I had enough good sense, or obstinacy, or something, to retain a subconscious belief that, inasmuch as books were meant to be read, good books ought to be interesting, and the best books capable in addition of giving one a lift upward in some direction. After a while it dawned on me that all of the conscientious, industrious, painstaking little pedants, who would have been useful people in a rather small way if they had understood their own limitations, had become because of their conceit distinctly noxious. They solemnly believed that if there were only enough of them, and that if they only collected enough facts of all kinds and sorts, there would cease to be any need hereafter for great writers, great thinkers. They looked for instance at Justin Winsor's conglomerate narrative history of America—a book which is either literature or science in the sense in which a second rate cyclopedia is literature and science—as showing an "advance" upon Francis Parkman—Heaven save the mark! Each of them was a good enough day laborer, trundling his barrowful of bricks and worthy of his hire; as long as they saw themselves as they were they were worthy of all respect; but when they imagined that by their activity they rendered the work of an architect unnecessary they became both absurd and mischievous. Unfortunately with us it is these small men who do most of the historic teaching in the colleges. They have done much real harm in preventing the development of students who might have a large grasp of what history should really be. . . . They are honestly unconscious that all they are doing is to gather bricks and stones, and that whether their work will or will not amount to anything really worthy depends entirely upon whether or not some great master builder hereafter arrives who will be able to go over their material, to reject the immense majority of it, and out of what is left to fashion some edifice of majesty and beauty instinct with the truth that both charms and teaches. . . .

There—I have not been able to deny myself the pleasure of writing you this wholly irrelevant letter. . . . good by and good luck.

Faithfully yours,
Theodore Roosevelt

*From *The Letters of Theodore Roosevelt*, Vol. 3, Elting E. Morison, ed., Harvard University Press, 1951